W9-BEU-125

THE AGENDA MOVER

THE BLG *PRAGMATIC LEADERSHIP* SERIES

THE AGENDA MOVER

When Your Good Idea Is Not Enough

SAMUEL B. BACHARACH

A BLG Book
Published in Association with Cornell University Press
ITHACA AND LONDON

First published 2016 by BLG Books in Association with Cornell University Press

Design by Scott Levine

Library of Congress Cataloging-in-Publication Data

Names: Bacharach, Samuel B., author.
Title: The agenda mover : when your good idea is not enough / Samuel B. Bacharach.
Description: Ithaca : A BLG Book published in association with Cornell University Press, 2016. | Series: The BLG pragmatic leadership series | Includes bibliographical references.
Identifiers: LCCN 2016010765 | ISBN 9781501710001 (cloth : alk. paper)
Subjects: LCSH: Leadership. | Organizational behavior. | Management. | Success in business.
Classification: LCC HD57.7 .B3215 2016 | DDC 658.4/092--dc23
LC record available at http://lccn.loc.gov/2016010765

Contents

CONTENTS

Preface

Leaders are not remembered for their dreams, aspirations, or intentions. They are remembered because they moved agendas. Ideas and visions don't necessarily make someone a leader, and neither do charm and personality. Brilliant ideas are a great starting point, and charisma and charm are fine, but leadership means being able to get things done. Leadership is not simply about having an agenda but having the pragmatic skills to move that agenda.

A lot of people talk a good game. A lot of people have great ideas. How to reduce health care costs? How to install a new IT system that will make the Nebraska division more profitable? How to provide alternative energy? How to expand your capacity in the field of biometric scanning software? Great ideas are the backbone of change and innovation. A great idea without execution, however, is hallucination. Your efforts at creating change and being innovative and entrepreneurial depend on your ability to go the distance and achieve results. Everyone can dream, but leaders go beyond the dreams and move agendas. Agenda movers are pragmatic leaders who know how to get into a campaign mindset, mobilize support around their idea or agenda, negotiate the buy-in, and sustain their initiative to implementation.

Agenda movers know how to mobilize support around an agenda while sustaining momentum to ensure results.

PREFACE

Creativity and good ideas are abundant. Everyone's had a brilliant idea. While creativity isn't scarce, what is in short supply are the people who have the skills to turn creative, innovative ideas into concrete realities.

Large companies and small businesses come up with hundreds if not thousands of new ideas every year. While ideas are ubiquitous— the proverbial "dime a dozen"—only a handful see the light of day.

If creativity, good ideas, and new insights are going to have consequences and result in real products, innovations, and true change, then organizations—large and small, corporate and nonprofit—need pragmatic leaders who have the ability to move things forward to create lasting change.

Agenda movers make decisions, take action, and create change. They have the capacity to take ideas and make them happen. Put simply, leaders who are agenda movers have the competence to rally people behind an idea and sustain forward movement to get results. Regardless of the quality of your idea and the appeal of your charm, if you lack this competence, you are not leading. If you think about leaders who have stood the test of time and continue to be admired today, you will see that they were pragmatists who knew how to sustain their campaign to achieve results. These leaders understood that their leadership wasn't sustained by having flair or great sound bites but by keeping the focus and having the skills to go the distance.

Without these skills, your most brilliant innovation, your best-laid plan will get stuck in the quagmire of inertia, in the muck of repetition, in the doldrums of inaction. Your dreams will become delusions, and your agenda will be nothing more than talk.

The leadership challenge of moving an agenda can present itself at any level of the organization, from the president's office to the mail room. If you have a project that needs to happen, if you're backing an innovation that is meeting resistance, if you want to push change in your organization, then you are called upon to lead. And to lead, you have to be an agenda mover, being mindfully aware of the intentions of others and mastering the pragmatic skills necessary to execute.

Acknowledgments

A number of years ago, I learned an important lesson—the true test of academic ideas is in practice. Like many ideas, good or bad, this book has traveled the maze from academia to the world of practice, from the classroom to the workplace. As an academic, I've learned that our core ideas remain with us, but evolve. This volume is a culmination of a long journey, from my books with Ed Lawler, such as *Power and Politics in Organizations* and *Bargaining, Power, Tactics, and Outcomes* to my later books like *Get Them on Your Side* and *Keep Them on Your Side*. I would like to thank my colleagues and friends who have seen me on this journey. I am grateful to my New York City Cornell intern students who participate in my Monday afternoon workshops.

The experience I've had working with my colleagues at the Bacharach Leadership Group (BLG) training leaders in organizations around the world, from high tech to higher education, has allowed me to be grounded in the world of execution rather than the world of theory. This book is testimony to those important insights we learned together.

Many key individuals have helped this process and deserve acknowledgment. Gianpaolo Barozzi, Senior Director, HR, at Cisco, has worked with BLG in what has become a truly productive collaboration; Ted Dodds explicitly understood the ideas and relevance of the ideas in this volume for many industries, especially IT; Andy Doyle, CHR at OppenheimerFunds, has helped focus many of these practical ideas; Robert Rothman, Senior Vice President, Wealth Management at UBS Financial Services, Inc., shared his knowledge; Mary Opperman, Vice President for Human Resources at Cornell University, was an early advocate for the application of our ideas to higher education; Chris Proulx, CEO of LINGOs, has been a superb sounding board over the last several years; Paul Salvatore, Partner at Proskauer, has been a great supporter and tremendous teaching partner; Kimberly Weisul, Editor-at-Large at *Inc.*, has been generous in sharing her wealth of knowledge and helping making BLG's ideas relevant to women leaders and entrepreneurs; Kathleen Weslock, EVP and Chief People Officer at Frontier Communications, has long appreciated and supported many of the efforts that led to the development of this volume; and Dana Vashdi, a team leadership expert, academic colleague, and BLG Affiliate Trainer, has been generous with her insights.

I am especially grateful to two of my students: Winston Feng, now Investment Professional at Point72 Asset Management, and my current Research Assistant, Napoleon Zapata. The input of Bryan Dominguez, Suzanne Shah-Hosseini, Saaylee Potnis, and William Moore has been especially helpful. The friendship of Chris Smithers and the political insights of Elmira Mangum, President of FAMU, fortified these efforts. My lunch discussions with Fran Bonsignore have been learning experiences. I am grateful to my support network at Cornell, including Esta Bigler, Jack Goncalo, Robert Smith, Dan McCray, and Bill Sonnenstuhl.

I am deeply grateful for Peter Bamberger's support and collaboration over the last thirty years. Harry Katz and Ed Lawler shared their street smarts. Finally, I am most appreciative to all those people who have been through BLG training programs, whose input has improved the quality of not only our training but also this book. From India to RTP, to Milan, Tel Aviv, Beijing, and Geneva, their input and generosity of spirit is greatly appreciated.

My colleagues at BLG have been partners in this effort. Two superb Senior BLG Affiliate Trainers, Kathy Burkgren and Chris Halladay, have really helped hone these ideas for higher education.

In particular, at BLG, I am especially grateful to James Briggs, Project Coordinator and Learning Designer, whose singularity of focus has not only assisted with this volume but also has been a major reason for much of our success.

I want to thank my friends and colleagues at Cornell University Press, who had the courage to take on this series: Nathan Gemignani for his outreach; Ange Romeo-Hall for her focused editing; Scott Levine for his aesthetic minimalism; the visionary head of the Press, Dean Smith; and Fran Benson, a colleague of many years who is a superb developmental editor.

Katie Briggs, my longtime friend and colleague, has again added her wisdom, her editorial touch, and her common sense to make this book possible. Katie has been instrumental to whatever success my career has achieved over the last decade. BLG's Training Director, Yael Stark Bacharach, with her understanding of team leadership and team coaching, has contributed not only her critiques and ideas but also her leadership to BLG. Finally, I want to thank my son, Ben for his appreciation of leadership.

THE AGENDA MOVER

1

THE POLITICAL COMPETENCE OF EXECUTION

DON'T RELY ON THE POWER OF YOUR IDEA...

It's often said that leaders achieve success because of their great ideas or irresistible vision.

Was George Washington the only military-minded man who believed in American independence? Was Martin Luther King Jr. the first African American to dream of race equality in America? Was Sam Walton the first man to believe in selling products at low cost?

Of course not. Good ideas and vision certainly helped these leaders keep focus, but their initial idea wasn't the sole reason for their success. These leaders succeeded because they had the pragmatic, political skills to get people to rally around their idea and work to make it a reality.

Jack Dorsey, founder of Twitter and Square, notes, "Everyone has an idea. But it's really about executing the idea . . . and attracting other people to help you work on the idea."[1]

This is the dilemma all leaders face. Once they have a viable idea, they need the skills to get people involved so they can turn that idea into a reality.

Jeff Bezos would agree. In August 2013 Bezos bought the *Washington Post* for $250 million. In his first interview after the purchase, Bezos said something that all leaders and entrepreneurs should pay close attention to:

> In my experience, the way invention, innovation and change happen is [through] team effort. There's no lone genius who figures it all out and sends down the magic formula. You study, you debate, you brainstorm and the answers start to emerge. It takes time. Nothing happens quickly in this mode. You develop theories and hypotheses, but you don't know if readers will respond. You do as

many experiments as rapidly as possible. "Quickly" in my mind would be years.[2]

Bezos maintains that there is no such thing as a lone genius who comes up with a magic formula. He says innovation only gets implemented after team effort, development, and testing.

Good leaders don't spend their days dreaming. They spend most of their time building coalitions of support around their idea. If you build a good base of support, implementation will follow.

As you know, having an idea or a vision is only the beginning. Ultimately, leadership is about execution—and to execute there are a series of steps you as a leader need to take. There is no big mystery about execution. The skills of execution are attainable and achievable.

Your success as a leader will be evaluated on whether you are able to take your vision and ideas and turn them into concrete reality. You will be judged not on your creative ideas but by your ability to make sure your ideas result in solid innovation, a new product, or better process. It isn't the vision of a new policy, program, or product that matters, but the executed policy, program, or product. The premise of pragmatic leadership is that your accomplishments count more than your aspirations.

...OR CHARISMA

The nineteenth-century sociologist Max Weber was the first to emphasize the importance of charisma as a key leadership attribute. For Weber, charisma is a deeply rooted personality trait that enables certain individuals to command others by the sheer power of their presence. Charisma suggests a mystical bond between leader and followers, with the latter defining their aspirations and in some cases their values by those of the former. As such, charisma, for Weber, is a crucial ingredient in the mix of qualities that make for successful, productive leaders.

Weber's view is that leadership is the property of a select, charismatic few. Leadership is an elitist gift that some possess and others simply do not and cannot. As Bob Knight, the controversial long-time coach of the University of Indiana and Texas Tech basketball teams, once told a group of business students, "The first thing you people need to know about leadership is that most of you simply do not have it in you."[3]

When you are in a crowd listening to a charismatic leader, what do you think? If you subscribe to Weber's mystical, superheroic notion of leadership, if you believe in the inspirational drama of charisma, what you're probably thinking is, "That ain't me." And by the cultural glorification of charisma, society tells most people, at least when it comes to leadership, "That ain't you." Do not listen. This voice is nothing less than license to evade responsibility. When leadership is a trait possessed by the few, who can blame the ordinary mortal when things don't work out? You have an automatic out: "What do you expect? I'm not a leader."

At a September 2005 congressional hearing, former Federal Emergency Management Agency director Michael Brown was grilled about his organization's poor response in helping the victims of Hurricane Katrina. Brown's response is the epitome of self-justification: "You want me to be this superhero!"[4]

Brown's defense encapsulates everything that is wrong with the cultural notion of charismatic leadership. Brown wasn't supposed to be a superhero. Nobody expected him to be. He just needed to move people out of the Superdome. He didn't fail because he lacked charisma. He failed because he wasn't an agenda mover.

Agenda movers know that in the final analysis charisma doesn't move the trucks.

The fact that some charismatic people are leaders doesn't mean that charisma is a litmus test of leadership. Bill Gates, Jeff Bezos, Dwight Eisenhower, and many others demonstrate that leaders are defined by their actions and by their ability to execute a plan—not by their charismatic personalities.

Take Bill Gates. Uncharismatic as they come, he has the prototypical introspective, computer-geek personality—yet he's one of the richest men in the world, and undoubtedly one of the most influential. Gates calls himself a "geek"[5]—a word that doesn't suggest all the social graces but implies that he is packed full of curiosity. Being a geek did not prevent Gates from pushing his idea into offices and households worldwide. While Gates isn't the only geek building and selling software, he is an effective leader who created a global business empire by getting things done.

Amazon's Jeff Bezos also lacks the traditional trappings of charisma. He looks like an everyday guy, but his passion for what he calls Amazon's Leadership Principles shines through. These values—an obsession with customers, ownership, a bias for action, frugality, a high hiring bar, and innovation—are the foundation of his success. Bezos built an organization with a strategic vision and a culture dedicated to execution. He may not stand out in a crowd, but can you think of a more effective leader?

John Kenneth Galbraith characterized the Eisenhower presidency (1953–1961) as "the bland leading the bland."[6] Yet his leadership was more than that. Likable, but hardly charismatic, Eisenhower was principled, proactive, and pragmatic. While unlikely to come up with brilliant insights, he could look at a problem, analyze it, assess available alternatives, and choose among them. Eisenhower said, "Pull the string and it will follow wherever you wish. Push it, and it will go nowhere at all."[7] He knew getting things done is about more than a sheer force of will. It's about pulling people into groups, coalitions, and teams.

During World War II Eisenhower observed, "In a war such as this, when high command invariably involves a president, a prime minister, six chiefs of staff, and a horde of lesser 'planners,' there has got to be a lot of patience—no one person can be a Napoleon or a Caesar."[8] Eisenhower knew the value of patience and that coalitions and political sway were necessary then—and are necessary now—to accomplishing a complex mission.

Getting things done within the framework of a coalition is a slow process, and Eisenhower relied on patience and humility. Eisenhower didn't storm around and demand that everything be done his way and on his timetable.

There are very few Napoleons or Caesars in modern organizations. Leaders need to work with others and build coalitions if they want to get things done. They can't simply sit back, mandate, and expect that their desires will be fulfilled.[9]

Nearly half a century after Ike, Mark Zuckerberg, founder of Facebook, echoed this theme: "I believe that over time, people get remembered for what they build, and if you build something great, people don't care about what someone says about you . . . they care about what you build."[10]

Agenda movers know that in the final analysis, charisma on its own doesn't get a lot done. Leadership comes down to execution.

LEAD WITH A SMALL "L"

Leadership on the basis of grand ideas or the cult of charisma and personality may have its place—this is leadership with a big "L." Big ideas and big personality. It may be a perfectly fine way of initially mobilizing a group of individuals and getting a focus on an agenda, but to truly move ahead and create change, leaders need to be focused and mindful while using tactical pragmatic skills to make sure that the desired results are achieved.

This is leadership with a small "L"—leadership based on specific behavioral microskills embedded in a leader's managerial and political competence.

When thinking of great figures in history such as Abraham Lincoln, you can marvel about Lincoln's capacity to be aware of others, focus on an agenda, and to know what behaviors would elicit the support and would ensure the continuity of his ideas. Leaders like Lincoln are mindful of their behavioral skills.

If you look at late Steve Jobs's amazing career, one thing becomes apparent: Jobs was a man who could get things done. This was the primary leadership skill from which his success flowed. Jobs succeeded because he knew how to make things happen. He knew whom he needed to spend his time with, how to identify and categorize his priorities, and how to manage the people who would do the day-to-day work of designing great products.

Jobs's galvanizing personality is still being dissected in the popular press. While his stage presence can teach public speakers a thing or two, and his passion can show young entrepreneurs that energy is essential to business, his leadership skills fade into the background. Jobs is viewed as the confident, passionate chief executive officer of Apple. The fact that he had to develop a very specific set of microskills to move agendas is overlooked.

Jobs knew that innovation and creativity aren't necessarily fueled by throwing dollars into research. Jobs knew that it wasn't about the money. Rather, it was about having quality people and understanding that success means executing plans and producing results.

Jobs said just that: "Innovation has nothing to do with how many R&D dollars you have. When Apple came up with the Mac, IBM was spending at least 100 times more on R&D. It's not about money. It's about the people you have . . . and how much you get it."[11]

Jobs was successful because he was proactive and pragmatic in pushing his ideas. His charisma helped shape who he was but was not essential to his program. He understood what was possible and knew how to get it done. He understood leadership with a small "L"—and that it is encapsulated in the microskills of execution.

Martin Luther King Jr. is another charismatic leader who is remembered because of his accomplishments, not only because of his personality. While King's popular image is propped up by moments of oratorical eloquence, these moments were relatively few. King wasn't always preaching. Like Jobs, he spent most of his time dealing with the pragmatic day-in-day-out strategic issues involved in moving his agenda forward. For King, that meant organizing communities, knowing who his allies were, knowing where his support was weak, knowing where his support was strong, and understanding what needed to be done to sustain forward movement.

He was constantly evaluating and reevaluating. One of King's great moments, the March on Washington for Jobs and Freedom, at which he delivered his "I Have a Dream" speech, took immense organization. Among myriad other things, King consulted extensively with President John F. Kennedy to ensure there would be protection for the demonstrators. While his speech is rightly remembered and celebrated, the planning and hard work that took place behind the scenes are largely forgotten.

King said, "Ultimately, a genuine leader is not a searcher for consensus but a molder of consensus."[12] Leaders don't scramble in a search for consensus—they make it. Leadership is about building a group of supporters—that is, a coalition that can help turn your innovative idea into a reality.

King, like Jobs, appreciated leadership with a small "L." For him, leadership was not a function of rhetoric, personality, or vision, but of the focused, deliberate, pragmatic steps that led to true accomplishment. What Jobs and King share with all effective leaders is an unerring sense of the practical and an appreciation of the pragmatic. Both had dreams, but both also clearly recognized that nothing would change unless they engaged in a focused campaign to make it happen. They knew that their success was dependent on their ability to move things forward. Without their practical skills of pragmatic leadership, their dreams would have never got off the ground and changed the lives of millions.

BUILD A COALITION

If you're a lone ranger—that is, if you're one of those individuals who prefer to rely solely on your own skills, knowledge, and intelligence—you lose out on vitally important resources: the skills, knowledge, and intelligence of others. To succeed, you need to harness what others have to offer. This means you need to campaign to get others in your corner and keep them there. Your goal is to build collective support.

Even leaders in powerful positions forget this important lesson. Take Woodrow Wilson, the twenty-eighth president of the United States (1913–1921). Clearly he had leadership ability and was a visionary of the first order—but he wasn't always successful—especially during his tenure as president of Princeton University.

In 1902, Francis L. Patton retired as president of Princeton University, arguably the most elite American university of that era. The board of trustees turned to a young political scientist, Thomas

Woodrow Wilson, to take over.

Wilson was a popular choice and had many innovative ideas on how to make the university better in both the academic and social spheres. He successfully implemented several educational reforms, created new academic departments, directed the undergraduate study program, and developed the widely acclaimed preceptorial system, whereby students become more actively engaged in their studies by having regular meetings with professors. Yet some of Wilson's most ambitious ideas fell apart and ultimately derailed his presidency because he neglected to anticipate the resistance his ideas would face. He failed to realize that good ideas aren't enough.

Wilson wanted to weaken the popular elitist eating clubs and create a more egalitarian campus. He felt that abolishing these dining cliques would create a more scholarly climate. While promising the Princeton community greater academic cohesion and social equality, the idea didn't wash with M. Taylor Pyne, an alumni and wealthy trustee of the university. Pyne loathed the idea of abolishing Princeton's exclusive eating clubs and threatened to withdraw his financial support of the school.[13]

While Wilson rested on the strength and moral superiority of his ideas, Pyne got to work. His first order of business was befriending Andrew West of the graduate school. West was a known critic of Wilson and was bristling at the president's plan to build the new graduate school near the undergraduate campus. While Wilson dreamed of the incubation and crossfertilization of ideas that would take place if the undergraduate and graduate schools were located closer to each other, West saw the schools' close proximity as a calamity. He wanted peace, quiet, and seclusion and didn't want to be forced to rub shoulders with a young, restless student body. Between them, Pyne and West had much to grumble about and a lot of political clout. The controversy divided the trustees and faculty into two factions: one that agreed with Wilson and one that opposed his radical ideas.

Ultimately, the university had no choice but to go with Pyne's money and West's appeals over Wilson's ideals. Wilson was compelled to resign. His groundbreaking ideas, in isolation, were not enough to carry the day. Wilson failed to anticipate how his innovative ideas would be received by key stakeholders at the university. Wilson's principal aim was to change the culture of the university, but he failed to recognize the broader ramifications of his plan. In the end, he was stymied by a determined and organized opposition.

As president of the United States, Wilson once again came up with a pioneering idea. In 1919, he presented to the American public his famed Fourteen Points, which introduced the notion of a League of Nations, an international body intended to prevent another world war. By all measures, the proposed League was a good idea, but Wilson failed to get his own country on board. The League eventually dissolved not for lack of noble purpose but because Wilson was unable to move an agenda. Wilson faltered in choosing his audience and articulating his message. He failed to be pragmatic. He did not internalize the primary lesson of the agenda mover: get those whom you need on your side and keep them there.

As an agenda mover you understand that decisions can be imperfect. However diligent and methodical you may be, you're going to have some blind spots. Agenda movers acknowledge that their decision making is bounded, constrained by their ability, their knowledge, and their available resources. Further, they know that they see the world from their own perspective. Agenda movers are aware that their self-interest, emotions, cognitive capacity, and background can trip them up if they are not careful and that being smart is not a guarantor of success. Regardless of how detailed the PowerPoint presentation, in a world of perpetual uncertainty, no plan is ever going to be perfect. Being aware of their own limitations, and of the uncertainty around them, and appreciating the vulnerability of any decision, especially those involving innovation and change, pragmatic leaders focus on building collective support.

Building a coalition gives you an opportunity to exchange ideas with others and to fine-tune your plan, both initially and as you go forward. Having a coalition also lends legitimacy to your agenda. The more people you have on your side, the more legitimate your agenda will appear to others. Having a coalition enhances your capacity to meet challenges from your opponents and to stand up against detractors and critics. It is harder to derail an agenda that has a firm foundation of collective support.

Consider the coalition formed by eight states, including California, New York, and Massachusetts, to join forces to promote the sale and use of electric cars. The coalition members have agreed to install more electric charging stations, offer tax incentives for electric car users, and set targets for having more zero-emission vehicles on their roads. By partnering together, the coalition represents 23 percent of the U.S. auto market and intends to overcome the barriers that have thus far impeded the growth of electric cars.[14]

The coalition not only provides a forum for its member states to exchange ideas about the best technology available but also communicates the importance of the issue to other stakeholders. Although time will tell if the eight governors will keep their coalition intact, a similar coalition was formed in the early 1990s in an effort to enact more restrictive emission limits, which was a success in its own right and was later mirrored by the federal government.[15]

When you are moving change, when you are driving innovation, when you are rolling out a new program, you are leading a campaign for support. You cannot assume that the grandeur of your insight or the grace of your personality will gain you that support. If you want others to rally around your ideas, you must involve yourself in the nitty-gritty of a campaign. How you go about leading the campaign to gain the necessary support will determine whether you are a leader who can move agendas or simply a dreamer.

To lead this campaign for innovation and change, you need to develop the core competencies of pragmatic leadership. You need the political skills required to build a coalition and the managerial skills required to sustain forward movement.

An agenda mover understands that there are four major stages in any campaign. First, you must anticipate the agendas of others, being mindfully aware of their intentions and aspirations. You must interpret their objectives, map the political landscape, figure out how you'll sell your ideas, and prepare for resistance. Second, you must mobilize your campaign. You must focus your message, justify your agenda, and establish your credibility in order to gain initial support. Third, you must negotiate the buy-in. That is, having established initial support, you must come to a concrete understanding that others are truly in your corner and committed to a common agenda. Fourth, you must sustain momentum. That is, create traction, stay agile, and maintain a campaign mind-set. You must manage your team to ensure results and go the distance.

Whether you are trying to centralize IT, get funding for a start-up, get support from up top for a new idea, change the compensation system, push a new health care policy, champion civil rights or environmental reform, relocate your offices to the fifth floor, or put in a new human resources information system, the rules of the game are the same. You can't act alone. You have to campaign for innovation and change.

The rest of this book will break down leadership into the core competencies you need to anticipate, mobilize, negotiate, and sustain a campaign. Each stage has delineated and specific behavioral skills. You will learn to develop these skills to initiate and sustain a campaign for change. In short, you will learn how to be a pragmatic leader capable of moving any agenda.

2

ANTICIPATE THE AGENDAS OF OTHERS

Know Where They're Coming From

ANTICIPATE

Anticipation is a critical but unheralded leadership skill. Too often, people just blurt out their ideas or suggestions without being mindfully aware of either the context or the agendas of others. Agenda movers know that once they say something, the genie is out of the bottle—and all the wishing in the world isn't going to make it go back in. The challenge for a leader who aspires to be an agenda mover is to be aware of how other people may receive their ideas and suggestions. In every setting, but especially in organizations, any action has implications that might not be immediately obvious. Your agenda, no matter how innocuous, could have an impact on the resources, ambitions, and goals of others.

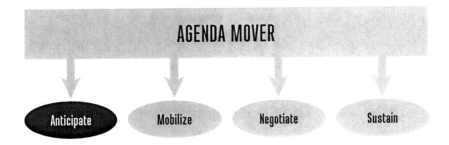

When you are trying to innovate and create change, your idea inevitably is going to have an impact on others—especially when resources are scarce. When moving your idea ahead, you have to make sure that it isn't stifled before you get a fair hearing. You have to anticipate the reaction of others. Indeed, one aspect of political competence that is often overlooked is empathy—that is, putting yourself in the shoes of others to understand where they are coming from. Without this capacity, it is unlikely you will gain the support you need to achieve lasting results.

In trying to move innovation and create change, the lack of anticipatory skills can trip up the unprepared leader. Such a leader might think everyone is on board but is caught off guard by unforeseen resistance. It's a safe bet that a leader in this situation neglected to map the agendas of others and figure out potential allies and resistors. This is a mistake that pragmatic agenda movers rarely make.

Every new idea follows the principles of physics—that is, every new idea elicits some reaction. The reaction might be subtle, perhaps barely perceptible, but there will be one. You have to consider how the new idea affects those you need in your corner.

To move your agenda ahead, you need to know whom you're dealing with, interpret intentions, gauge their resistance, and, if resistance is high, you need to anticipate what arguments they will make against your initiative.

Know Whom You're Dealing With

To determine what kind of effect your action will have, it's crucial to understand the dynamics of turf and power. Are new ideas welcomed by your organization, institution, or group? Or are new ideas greeted with suspicion? Think about your idea in the context of the power dynamics of your organization. Are key stakeholders threatened by your idea? Why? Do they like your idea? Why? The key to understanding the impact of new ideas is your capacity to clarify the needs and intentions of stakeholders.

Map the Stakeholders

Agenda movers appreciate that organizations are not harmonized bodies. Organizations are made up of individuals, and however well those individuals work together in pursuit of the collective good, there is a natural divergence of perspectives, needs, and goals. In the organizational context, individuals and groups differ in their intentions, even with regard to common goals. Organizations are political systems. In trying to move change and innovation, you must first classify the stakeholders.

Top Dogs

Top Dogs are the organizational decision makers, those with official authority and veto power. All organizational activity happens on their watch. To paraphrase Harry Truman, the buck stops with them. Top Dogs have the authority to approve decisions—and to torpedo them.

Top Dogs may choose to act or not to act. They may be passive or proactive. Ultimately, they have the capacity to dictate what happens and what doesn't. Some small ideas can be implemented without the approval of the Top Dog, but without their support, bigger ideas will wither on the vine.

Smaller organizations typically have one Top Dog. But you might find multiple Top Dogs in a larger organization, especially if the central power position is ceremonial in nature.

Gatekeepers

Gatekeepers have segmented authority. That is, they have authority over a limited set of issues, and they liaison between the Top Dog(s) and the rest of the organization. Though Gatekeepers are formally under the supervision of the Top Dog, they are often left alone to make decisions that fall within their purview. The Gatekeeper might be an individual, but typically Gatekeepers are found in a group, like senior management or the finance committee.

Gatekeepers are going to want a full look at your initiative before helping to move it forward. You should be as cooperative as you can be with Gatekeepers. Other stakeholders heed the opinions of the Gatekeepers and will be more likely to join you if they know the Gatekeepers are on board.

Gurus

Gurus are organizational actors who are not involved in the daily life of the organization. They can be senior individuals with a unique perspective, such as external consultants, the board of directors, or others who have influence with the decision makers. External consultants can be a sounding board for senior management when discussing new ideas.

Be aware of others in the organization who can weigh in on virtually any issue, such as a chief of staff. These individuals, though on the periphery, have influence because of their unique position in the organization. Gurus may be difficult to identify and even more difficult to map accurately. Making yourself aware of their presence is an important step toward managing the influence they have with others in your organization.

Players

Players are influential stakeholders whose specific activities will be directly impacted by your initiative. They are perhaps your most challenging constituency. While Players do not have broad formal authority, their influence comes from their deep understanding of the specific activities and technologies necessary to get the job done. Players make things happen.

You will find that Players will be your most vocal detractors—and also your strongest supporters. Be very careful not to discount Players. Make sure to give them the attention they deserve. An overlooked or ignored Player can become your harshest critic.

It is important to remember that Players far outnumber Top

Dogs, Gatekeepers, and Gurus. When thinking about the Players in your organization, don't forget to include your direct reports and subordinates. Don't assume that they will go along with your intent simply because you're the boss or have a measure of authority. You need to keep the Players that you supervise engaged as you move forward. They will be integral to your success once your initiative gets off the ground.

▲ ▲ ▲

Use this classification system to identify some of the key stakeholders who might be impacted by your initiative. Take the example of a university. The president and the board of trustees are the Top Dogs—they hold the final authority. They have the power to overturn any decision. Under the president and board is a maze of Gatekeepers—the department chairs, vice presidents, and deans who manage most of the day-to-day decision making. There are Gurus—the consultants, senior faculty members, retired trustees, successful alumni, and donors. Last, there are the Players—faculty with research agendas, program heads, and teaching assistants.

Imagine you are a well-established faculty member with a proposal for a new business major. You've noticed that the university has slipped in the national rankings, and you believe that to remain competitive, your institution has to offer this new major. You think that research in this area will not only bring academic acclaim but will also attract top-notch faculty and better applicants. With new faculty and highly qualified, talented students, the university's rankings will undoubtedly rise—not to mention the potential for a subsequent spike in donations.

To get your change and innovation campaign off the ground and move your idea forward, you need to anticipate how your idea may alter the dynamics of the university. You might need seed funding from the dean. Where is the money going to come from? It will probably be taken from another program. How will this affect the number and quality of applicants for other majors? Will they slip? Will the salaries of other faculty be affected? Will prestigious new faculty be better paid than current faculty? Will the new major affect grants and contracts? Will there be new opportunities for outside funding? How will the new major affect the established culture of the university?

While your goal is to benefit the university overall and to provide more options for students, remember that your idea will affect everyone else at the university, at least tangentially. If you truly believe in your initiative, you also must know whom you need to target as you weave through the university maze to implement the new major.

Your challenge is to identify the Top Dogs, Gatekeepers, Gurus, and Players and determine how to use them in moving your change and innovation forward. Asking people for the wrong kind of support or pleading for help when their hands are tied is a misuse of your time and energy. If you waste time trying to convince the wrong people, you could jeopardize your entire change effort.

If you take your time, do your homework, classify the stakeholders, and understand how their support can enhance your agenda, you will be better equipped to bring them on board and allow them to make a meaningful contribution.

By classifying key stakeholders in the organization—whether a firm, university, community group, or anything else—you will have a better idea not only of where you stand but also of the type of support you most need to pursue. For example, if you're a Player, you'll likely work up the organizational ladder to recruit a number of Gatekeepers. If you're a Gatekeeper, you might need only one or two fellow Gatekeepers to achieve the same kind of institutional support. If you're a Top Dog, you still need people on your side, but you have more flexibility in recruiting others. You might seek out the endorsement of a Guru or recruit several Gatekeepers for support. In all these cases, you'll also want the support of key Players, who form the substrata of your organization and who, ultimately, are the people who will make your initiative work.

Decipher Power

As you classify the key stakeholders, you'll find yourself asking one straightforward question: Who has the power? One individual? Several? A group? More than one group? Who wields sufficient power to make a difference in helping you move your change effort or implement your innovation?

The question of power is at the heart of any leadership challenge. Any leader who tries to move an agenda or create change will have to overcome resistance from others. Leaders need to identify the power holders who can help them move their agenda ahead. This isn't Machiavellian. This is the simple fact of organizational life. In moving your campaign to create change, you need some power-wielding actors in your corner.

While countless philosophers, businessmen, and politicians have pondered the meaning of power, power is simply someone's ability to get others to do something they would not have done on their own. There are numerous ways of getting people to do things, from hints to flattery to deception to reasoning to brute force—but whatever method is used, the moment you talk about getting someone to do something they might not have done otherwise, you're talking about power. Leadership is about getting people to do things. As such, power is essential.

Individuals and groups differ not only in the amount of power they hold but also in its type. In assessing the power dynamics of your organization, it's important to avoid overgeneralization. You need to differentiate authority from influence.

Authority means having the capacity to make a final decision based on hierarchy. Authority is being able to say "yes" or "no" to a given proposal. Authority is associated with the formal position that one holds in the organization. For any decision, authority is at the top of the pyramid.

Influence is more nuanced. Influence is multidirectional and derives not from a position in a hierarchy but from one's experience, expertise, networking, and ability to persuade. Influence is the capacity to sway others toward taking a particular action.

Influence is a game of persuading, coaxing, and negotiating. Authority is a game of hierarchy. Agenda movers are acutely aware of these two organizational games and appreciate the differences and overlap between them. It is essential to categorize stakeholders into those with authority and those with influence.

Obviously, Top Dogs have authority. Their yea or nay is essentially a final decision. That's a given. What isn't given, and is more subtle, is when you should reach out to the Top Dog. You have to be careful to time your approach to the Top Dog, striking a balance between too early and too late.

While it is wonderful to get public reinforcement of your intentions from the Top Dog, the Top Dog will rarely get involved in the minutiae of moving an agenda ahead. Some agenda movers make the mistake of spending a lot of energy seeking explicit support from the Top Dog, when a better use of their time would be to incorporate other key stakeholders.

When you want to pragmatically put a new change or innovation in place in your organization, make sure the Top Dog knows a bit about what you are trying to do, but don't expend a lot of resources and energy in getting the Top Dog's attention. Since the Top Dog will not do the actual work of moving your agenda forward, you need to first find other partners.

In thinking about whom to approach for initial support, you might want to start with the Gatekeepers. Gatekeepers have segmented authority, and their power over functions, products, and divisions is highly delineated. They are the first-line decision makers in their area. Think of the director of marketing or the regional head of a manufacturing unit. Neither has the clout of a Top Dog, but both have concrete knowledge and expertise that might be useful as you seek to move your agenda ahead. A further advantage of starting with Gatekeepers is that they are often regarded as having substantial legitimacy. Others in the organization perceive that Gatekeepers know what they are talking about. Having the support of Gatekeepers early in the process can validate the legitimacy of your change initiative. In short, an investment of time with Gatekeepers is well worth the effort. They have the positional authority to offer concrete support in implementing and executing your plan, and, when the time comes, they are well placed to put in a good word on your behalf with the Top Dog.

Gurus do not have the decision-making authority of the Top Dog, and they aren't necessarily as well connected as Gatekeepers, but they are valuable because of their ability to influence others in the organization. Influence can be just as important as authority. Use tact when approaching Gurus for support. When you reach out to a Guru, there is no guarantee that the contact will lead to support from Players, Gatekeepers, or the Top Dog. Consider how Gurus fit into the organizational dynamic. For instance, because Gurus are formally outside of the organizational structure, others may view them as a threat. If you are a Player, you risk being accused of going around the authority structure by going to a Guru first.

Dealing with Gurus is a delicate matter. Spend too much time with them, and you might be coded as a sycophant or intriguer. Spend too little time with them, and they may feel ignored or dis-respected—and in response, may try to subtly delegitimize your efforts. Because Gurus have ambiguous roles in the organization, they can sometimes have sensitive egos. Be careful how you handle them.

Players may not have the segmented authority of Gatekeepers or the hierarchal authority of the Top Dog, but you need Players in your corner. Because Players have diffuse influence throughout the orga-nization, they can support you on a day-to-day basis as you move your change effort or innovation forward. In fact, Players might be more important than Gurus. Gurus may get you over the boulders, but Players can help you maneuver around the little bumps in the road.

Support from Players is critical when the scope of your change effort is broad and you need to mobilize a coalition to move your agenda ahead. To get this support, you will have to convince Players that they'll benefit from your project. Keep in mind that Players can emerge from all levels of the organization—including your direct subordinates. Never, ever underestimate a Player. The Player is your essential ally. Without Players you might be able to initiate a pro-gram, but you'll never be able to implement it. Time spent with a Player is rarely wasted.

As an agenda mover, you'll appreciate the need to be respectful and cautious with those in authority. Be mindful of who calls the shots. At the same time, be ready to use the key actors and groups who have influence and who can help in the everyday work of moving a change and innovation effort forward. Be prepared to anticipate which influence and authority figures you will need on your side.

Interpret Intentions

By now, you have assessed the dynamics of your organization, analyzed the roles and positions of stakeholders, and determined what kind of support your agenda needs. You have identified the key actors—the Top Dog, Gatekeepers, Gurus, and Players. You have an appreciation of the intricate network of relationships in your organization and know which individuals with authority and influence you want on your side. You need to be mindful of the goals of others and have a sense of how they hope to achieve them. You have to understand their game plan. You have to understand their agenda. That means first understanding the goals they are pursuing and how they intend to accomplish those goals.

One of the mistakes people make in trying to understand the agendas of others is they get too concrete, too fast. They focus only on the empirical issue at hand. "The Republicans do not want to eliminate the inheritance tax." "The Democrats do not want to eliminate any entitlement programs." By concentrating only on the specific, concrete issue rather than the underlying intention of the agenda you might miss the entire point. It is difficult to persuade people on issues without a deep understanding of their underlying game plan.

Tinkerers versus Overhaulers

All people have goals. The word "goals" is shorthand for a complex array of motivating factors that inspire people to be open to change and willing to improve aspects of their lives or conditions around them. A goal can be large or small, but it has to be something that a person can feel that he or she can accomplish (with the proper resources and under the right conditions). Individuals, however, perceive their goals differently. Some people have very specific goals. They approach change cautiously, aiming for small, incremental improvements, and work within the framework of the status quo. Others have broader goals. They set their sights on the big picture and aim toward sweeping change—fundamental transformation, restructuring, and rebuilding. The former are tinkerers, the latter, overhaulers.

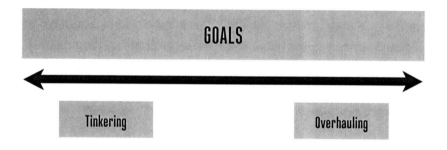

As you might imagine, both die-hard tinkerers and dedicated overhaulers tend to regard their goals as the only legitimate ones for the organization and see the opposing camp as flirting with disaster. Tinkerers argue that overhaulers move too fast, while overhaulers maintain that tinkerers are plodders and move too slowly. Tinkerers accuse overhaulers of panicking about missed windows of opportunity, while overhaulers reproach tinkerers for shifting the deck chairs on the Titanic. Tinkerers tell overhaulers that they underestimate the strength of the organization. Overhaulers fault tinkerers for ignoring reality.

Of course, these descriptions are somewhat misleading, in that it suggests that tinkerers and overhaulers occupy two distinct and nonoverlapping territories. In reality, the two stand at opposite ends

of a continuum. Most people fall somewhere between these extremes, depending on the circumstances. An overhauler likely will
not knock down his house and rebuild from scratch because the roof
leaks and the paint is fading. Still, the distinction between the types
is valid, and identifying where key stakeholders stand on this continuum is a useful exercise in the context of advancing an agenda.
For the agenda mover, the point of this exercise is not to determine
which type of goal is "right," but to build a supportive coalition. To
this end, it's important to know how to choose potential partners for
your coalition and how to market your idea in a way that will most
effectively win them over.

Just as there are differences between tinkering and overhauling
goals, there are differences in people's preferred style of execution—
how they go about getting things done. Some are planners while others are improvisers.

Planners versus Improvisers
Planners believe that it is within their power to ascertain most of the
issues, problems, and variables they will face in completing a project
or accomplishing a goal and that they will be able to predict, with
some accuracy, the likely outcomes and consequences of their decisions. A planner is not prepared for surprises and reacts poorly when
unexpected events arise. A planner is fairly confident that the future
is knowable. In a world of ambiguity and uncertainty, planners put
their trust in methodical analysis, step-by-step progressions, tight
control, and accountability. Planners strongly believe that through
calculation and synchronization, chaos can be avoided.

Improvisers believe that organizations, institutions, and everyday
life are too chaotic to be controlled by planning. They believe that
the future is unpredictable and that the conflicting forces inherent

in the universe cannot be properly analyzed and that it isn't worth the time to prepare for every possible contingency. Improvisers prefer to be agile and ready to react as events unfold.

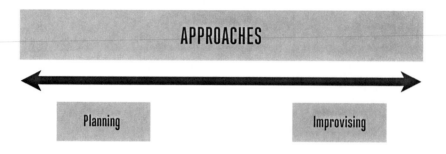

The improvisational approach is based on the assumption that individuals can minimize risk by building some give into the system that allows them to make changes as circumstances shift. Improvisers argue that there is no way of knowing what's around the corner, so there is no point in spending time and resources to prepare for every possible encounter up ahead. Instead, improvisers aim to pursue their agendas through fluid adaptation.

Focus on Their Agendas
Understanding the goals and problem-solving approaches of key actors gives you the critical dimensions you need to classify and analyze their personal attitudes toward change and progress—and helps you to understand their personal agendas. Combining the two goal-setting types (tinkerers and overhaulers) and the two execution approaches (planning and improvising) yields four different agendas that you, as an agenda mover, can use to assess potential coalition partners and identify individuals who are likely to resist your

plan for change. Are your potential partners traditionalists? Do they have a let's-be-careful mindset? Are they adjusters, who think they should cross the bridge when they come to it? Are they developers— ready to push the envelope but only within certain bounds? Or do they pursue a revolutionary agenda—and tear the envelope asunder? The four agenda archetypes are shown below.

THE FOUR AGENDA ARCHETYPES

	Tinkerer	Overhauler
Planner	traditionalist	developer
Improviser	adjuster	revolutionary

In identifying agendas of key stakeholders, you will doubtless find yourself asking similar questions about yourself. Before you approach others, it will be useful for you to explore your own natural mindset vis-à-vis change. Gaining insights into your own attitudes and propensities—understanding where you fit in the general scheme of things—will help you avoid conflict as you approach others. Remember, there is no absolute "right" or "wrong," although one approach may be better than another in a given situation.

The Let's-Be-Careful Traditionalist

Traditionalists are tinkerers and planners. Their goals are usually modest, and their strategies are organized and clear-cut. People with traditionalist agendas are ordinarily thought of as being conservative.

Traditionalists believe their role is to maintain stability even as others are charging full-steam ahead. They prefer making small changes, following precedent, and adhering to regimented process in achieving their goals. It is important to realize that despite their careful nature, traditionalists are neither inherently against change nor do they make poor leaders. They simply value order and routine.

While others skydive, a traditionalist is on the ground planning the landing reception. A traditionalist agenda leaves little room for error, meaning that traditionalists generally do not need abundant external scrutiny. In the organizational context, individuals with traditionalist agendas view growth and progress as taking place in stages, through careful planning and deliberate execution.

Warren Buffett, arguably one of the most successful financiers and a quintessential traditionalist, dispenses the following investment advice: "Be fearful when others are greedy, and be greedy when others are fearful." This adage exemplifies Buffett's belief that growth does not come through quick windfalls and that careful planning and execution are the keys to success. Buffett's performance following the 2008 financial crisis illustrates the benefits of a traditionalist approach. In 2008, as the credit markets tightened and panic among investors began to set in, Buffett became a prominent lender of capital to companies such as Goldman Sachs and Dow Chemical Co. Buffett's disciplined ability to forego short-term gains combined with his careful planning and execution strategy have materialized into $10 billion of earnings just five years following the crisis.[1] Warren Buffet is emblematic of the methodical nature often seen in traditionalists. He is widely regarded as the slow-and-steady leader of the financial markets. No drama, but consistency.

If you are a traditionalist, consider how other stakeholders are likely to react to an incremental, well-planned approach. Warren Harding was elected president of the United States (1921–1923) largely because of his campaign promise to return the country to "normalcy." Normalcy for Harding meant a return to the pre–World War I era, when the country wasn't enmeshed in bloody foreign conflicts or actively engaged in promoting progressive ideals. During the war years, the federal government grew in size and scope and Harding desired to turn back the clock. He saw his election as a mandate that the United States withdraw from the League of Nations. Under his polices, income tax rates were reduced, the economy improved, and unemployment fell. Harding took a traditionalist approach to help the nation recover some of its prewar prosperity. Historians tend to assess Harding kindly. His approach to change worked in the context of his times.

Traditionalists have the capacity to hunker down, be consistent, and move ahead at a steady pace. The drawback of this approach is that others can overtake them. Traditionalists might provide shelter in turbulent times, but sometimes they fail to capture an unanticipated opportunity and fail to stretch the envelope. The consistent nature of a traditionalist is a double-edged sword. Consistency can be a laudable quality, but consistency can also be an obstacle to innovation and change.

Another unexpected traditionalist is Henry Ford, founder of the modern automobile industry. In his autobiography, Ford recounted:

> Therefore in 1909 I announced one morning, without any previous warning, that in the future we were going to build only one model, that the model was going to be "Model T," and that the chassis would be exactly the same for all cars, and I remarked:
>
> "Any customer can have a car painted any colour (sic) that he wants so long as it is black."[2]

His insistence on one product and one color is music to the traditionalist's ears. Until the 1920s, Ford's strategy worked brilliantly. Shifting automobile ownership trends and high employee turnover, however, conspired to fundamentally shift the ruling dynamics within the automobile industry. Ford's response was to continue his old market-penetration strategy by doubling the hourly employee wage in an effort to decrease turnover and to increase employee performance motivation.

Ford's actions clearly illustrate the extent to which he believed that the problems he faced in 1920s mirrored those he tackled at the turn of the century. He did not take into account that two decades of automobile mass production saturated the market to the extent that automobile ownership trends began to shift. Consumers began viewing cars as a status symbol rather than a conveyance from point A to point B. They were looking to purchase vehicles that differentiated them from their neighbors. The standardization and mass production that made the Ford Motor Company successful in its early days worked against the company when customers were looking for more exciting products. Henry Ford's insistence on clinging to the familiar would cost him and his company dearly as the years progressed.

The Cross-That-Bridge-When-We-Come-to-It Adjuster

Like traditionalists, adjusters are conservative. Adjusters admit that some change might be needed but nothing too dramatic. They tinker in terms of their goals—but at the same time, their style is improvisational. They are likely to feel that the best plan is not to have one.

If you want to win over an adjuster, articulate as much as possible the conservative nature of your goals. If your goals are far-reaching, you might have to think about how to express them in terms of continuity rather than drastic change. In addition, show the adjuster that you are prepared to be flexible in terms of execution.

If you are an adjuster, consider how you market your plan to others. Tinkerers generally find that they meet lower levels of resistance, as their agendas do not have a drastic impact on the organization. On the other hand, an improvisational approach may be branded as too risky. If you've gained support for your overall plan, however, an improvisational approach allows for flexibility, meaning that changes may be easier to implement.

Yoon Boo-Keum, now president of Samsung Electronics, is a good example of a leader with an adjuster agenda. Yoon started his career with the company, had been a key player in its Visual Display Business since 2003, and was head from 2007–2011. He is a self-confessed adjuster, telling a reporter that he avoids meetings, and "prefer(s) to be in the field and make decisions on the spot."[3]

His support of LED TVs speaks to his adjuster nature. Sony launched the first LED TV in 2004, and Yoon noticed that the market gravitated toward this particular TV type, primarily owing to its enhanced energy efficiency. As a tinkerer, Yoon didn't invent something completely new but engineered a better design of a pre-existing product. Yoon moved decisively, and Samsung launched its first LED TV in 2009; now the company is a leader in this market. His support of LED TV, when this technology wasn't on the company's radar, illustrates Yoon's improvisation skill. Without a premeditated comprehensive plan to enter the LED TV market, his ability to be flexible allowed him to help Samsung react quickly to the growing popularity of LED TVs. Yoon is the quintessential adjuster.

In one of the biggest exercises in crisis management of all time, Treasury Secretary Henry (Hank) Paulson and Federal Reserve Chairman Ben Bernanke raced against the clock in late 2008 to save the U.S. financial system from ruin. As increasingly larger institutions found themselves in trouble, the team simply ran out of precedents and plans. Not since the Great Depression had a financial disaster of this magnitude taken place—and even then the government had failed miserably in reacting to the immediate aftermath of Black Tuesday. Yet Paulson and Bernanke's goal was unambiguously conservative: keep the economy afloat without nationalizing the banks. Circumstances forced them to adopt an adjuster agenda because they didn't know what surprises lurked around the corner.

As events unfolded, Paulson and Bernanke bailed out some banks while leaving others to go it alone. They improvised, hoping that each decision would result in a small boost to the financial system. It was the ultimate muddle-through, but their adjuster approach saved the country from a disastrous repeat of the crash of 1929.

The Push-the-Envelope Developer

Developers combine the characteristics of planners and overhaulers. They are committed to transformation, but their philosophy is that transformation can best be achieved through careful, methodical planning. They believe that thoughtful caution is the only sure defense against chaos.

Developers are grounded visionaries. Their goals have far-reaching consequences, but they take a planned, risk-averse approach. If you want to win over a developer, you will need to show that you've taken the possible consequences of your proposal into consideration and have prepared for setbacks and pitfalls. If you are a developer, you will need to win over two kinds of stakeholders: those who want limited change and those who want big changes, now.

The story of Kathy Giusti, founder and CEO of the Multiple Myeloma Research Foundation (MMRF), shows the strength of a developer agenda. MMRF was founded in 1996, the year that Giusti was diagnosed with Multiple Myeloma (MM), a rare life-threatening blood cancer. Creating the foundation was Giusti's attempt to apply her business acumen toward a cure. She was alarmed by the relative lack of treatment advancements—the options available to her were the same ones that her grandfather had when he was treated for the disease in 1956.[4] Giusti analyzed the situation and identified the factors that hindered MM treatment advancements. She discovered that the payoff for investing in MM research was not attractive enough for large pharmaceutical firms and that the researchers who did study the disease were not always willing to share results.

At first, MMRF operated as a grant-writing foundation. Generous donations, however, quickly allowed it to transform into a research foundation. Although she could not offer the monetary incentives that would entice large pharmaceutical firms to proceed with research, Giusti could develop and implement an incentive-based collaboration model that brought together scientists, research institutions, and diagnosed individuals. Within eighteen years, six MM drugs, developed under this model, have been FDA approved. Giusti's developer agenda, matched by her goals and detailed approach, allowed her and the MMRF to achieve great success.

Anne Mulcahy's tenure as CEO of Xerox exemplifies the strengths of a developer leading during challenging times. Soon after she became the CEO of Xerox, Mulcahy knew the company where she had spent twenty-five years of her career was in trouble. Mulcahy adopted a planned, risk-averse strategy that included continued investment in research and development, customer focus, and restructuring of its manufacturing and infrastructure, which she executed over an eight-year period. As CEO, Mulcahy was able to stave off bankruptcy and pressure from investors, clear Xerox of its $18 billion debt, and successfully emerge from an investigation by the Securities and Exchange Commission. By carefully taking the time to understand Xerox's financial and commercial positions, Mulcahy was able to not only restore Xerox's financial health but also transform its product and service offerings.[5]

Deng Xiaoping was a developer worth noting. When Deng succeeded Chairman Mao as leader of China's Communist Party (1978–1992), China had a closed, backward, collectivist economy. Deng's goal was to overhaul the economy and transform it into a free-market system while preserving the political agenda of the CCP. Deng started by forming limited special economic zones in production and export. When these early reforms showed a measure of success, he extended the model to other cities and rural areas. He introduced his initiative incrementally and deliberately, yet with an eye toward fundamental change. In doing so, Deng achieved market liberalization without dramatic social upheaval or runaway inflation. By using a developer approach, Deng successfully opened up China's economy and cleared the way for China to become a global powerhouse.

The Tear-the-Envelope Revolutionary

Revolutionaries, like developers, seek change that will fundamentally transform the mission and processes of the organization. But unlike developers, they want change now. They have no time for incremental steps. Indeed, revolutionaries believe that the health of the system depends on overturning its current operations. Because change headed by a revolutionary unfolds rapidly, it is impossible for them to work from—or even construct—a comprehensive plan in advance. Revolutionaries are willing to take on risk because they are agile and responsive, prepared to deal with events as they come.

Reed Hastings identified our love for film and television and our hatred for store lines, late fees, and due dates when he founded Netflix, but it was his capacity to continually transform Netflix that moved the organization from a DVD-by-mail service to a subscription-based, online streaming business with critically acclaimed original content whose membership out-performs its competitors.[6] As a revolutionary, Hastings's consistent focus on change and transformation of Netflix was both a blessing and a curse. While this revolutionary mind-set spurred Hastings to create Netflix, it also saw him act without first establishing a comprehensive plan. In 2011, Reed announced the spin-off of its DVD business and significant increases in membership rates. The backlash to this change was catastrophic—the share price plummeted and customers abandoned Netflix.[7] A true revolutionary, Hastings responded to these events (although without a plan) by apologizing to customers and constituents, focusing on improving the core business to restore faith in the organization, and ultimately venturing into original programming as a means to compete with cable networks and own and control its own content.[8]

Steve Jobs was a revolutionary—something that both hurt and helped his storied tenure with Apple. Jobs lost his position at Apple in 1985 because of his commitment to radical change and his tendency to improvise. He was brought back on board eleven years later because of those same attributes. During his two careers at Apple, Jobs helped pioneer the personal computing and electronics revolutions (the iPhone, iPod, iPad—and of course the Mac, which started it all).

Jobs was a revolutionary not only at Apple but also in the film industry. He acquired Pixar from George Lucas in 1986. Jobs had a vision to transform Pixar from a small computer graphics design company into a full-fledged film production company, but he had no specific plan for executing his idea. He invested $5 million in the company to keep it afloat, but there were no sure roads to success. Thus, he improvised.

First, Jobs introduced Pixar short-film animation projects that made little money but won industry acclaim and an Oscar, catching the attention of Disney. After muddling through many similar projects and some duds, Pixar successfully formed a partnership with Disney to create such hits as *Toy Story, Monsters, Inc., Finding Nemo,* and *Cars.* Full-feature computer animation, once considered impossible, is now standard in the film industry.

Ron Johnson, who is known as the brains behind the Apple Store and for making Target "cool," seemed like a natural to lead JCPenney. Arriving in early 2011 as CEO, Johnson immediately went to work to fundamentally transform the century-old firm. Within several months he proceeded to overhaul various structural and operational aspects, including improving store layouts and introducing full-but-fair pricing.[9] As it turned out, shoppers liked sales, coupons, and the illusion of finding a bargain. Johnson's vision flopped with customers. Consequently, the firm was forced to lay off more than 25 percent of its workforce, including a good chunk of the skilled workforce.[10]

For fiscal year 2012, sales revenues were disastrous. Johnson responded to the crisis by rescinding several organizational changes that he had initially instituted, including a return to the former (and previously successful) pricing strategy. Turning back the clock on some of the new changes was a case of too little, too late, and the stores lost more revenue.

Johnson attempted a complete overhaul JCPenney's organizational and operational structure, but his plans were not set in stone. He was completely willing to improvise and roll back the changes he instituted when things weren't working out. Johnson's tenure as the CEO of JCPenney illustrates not only how willing revolutionaries are to take on a program of transformational change but also how comfortable they are working without a net—that is, a firm plan of action. In his case, he was ultimately unsuccessful. Johnson himself was made redundant after seventeen months on the job.

In recent years there have been no shortage of revolutionaries, but as Hastings, Jobs, and Johnson show, they have the ability not only to stretch the envelope—but also to tear it asunder. In an organizational context, this can be problematic. Revolutionaries usually don't cultivate the grounded focus offered by traditionalists, adjusters, or even developers. While moving full-speed ahead, revolutionaries are in constant danger of falling off the cliff.

So Who's Who?

Being mindful of others' attitudes and approaches is crucial to building a campaign to create change, and the framework presented here offers a useful tool that can help you do that. Distinguishing traditionalists from developers, developers from adjusters, and adjusters from revolutionaries allows you to identify where others are coming from quickly and efficiently. In making these distinctions, be careful not to assume that these agendas are immutable or that people are uniformly consistent from one situation to another.

It would be great if a developer or a traditionalist could be spotted right away, but the reality is much more complex. The agenda archetypes presented here are not descriptions of personality. At most, they are general tendencies. While it is easy to classify individuals like Jobs and Deng into archetypes with predictable agendas, the attitudes and approaches of most people are fluid and highly dependent on the issue at hand. One can be a revolutionary in terms of recruitment but a traditionalist when it comes to budgeting.

When you're building a campaign, assessing stakeholders' archetypes can help you position yourself in relation to other people in your organization. Who are the traditionalists, developers, adjusters, and revolutionaries vis-à-vis the issue you want to change, and why? Without this focus, you are going to make assumptions about where other people stand without understanding why. Moreover, you can use this framework to better understand your own goals and approach in relation to the idea or issue in question. You can then use this self-understanding to better convince others why your plan is appropriate for the situation. Armed with this knowledge about others and yourself, you can figure out how to tailor your approach and how best to allocate your limited time and resources.

Map the Agendas of Others

As an agenda mover, you have to figure out how others see your agenda. By determining where people are coming from, you can estimate with some degree of accuracy how others will view your agenda. It is important to keep in mind that once a traditionalist does not mean always a traditionalist. If someone is a traditionalist, it might be only at this time and for this initiative. At other times—and for other issues, the same person might be a revolutionary, developer, or adjuster.

Before you move forward with your change effort, you have to map the agenda archetypes of others. The scenario below illustrates how mapping works.

Imagine that you are CEO of Endo Software, which supplies Software as a Service (SaaS) products to clients in the public utilities. Endo's products streamline back office operations, from human resources to equipment routing to risk management. The company was founded as an IT consulting firm but grew as a result of acquisitions. The result is that Endo is home to a motley collection of product teams, very few of which are fully integrated into the parent organization. The loosely coupled nature of the company allowed for quick expansion, and the product teams are largely entrepreneurial, rarely having to answer to anyone outside of their immediate group. The downside is that functions are frequently duplicated and some workers complain of the siloed natured of the organization.

With many municipalities facing tight budgets, pressure is rising within Endo to rationalize costs. You see this as a good opportunity to integrate the individual divisions from product verticals to functional verticals, reducing cost structure and increasing collaboration between teams. As a first step, you want to reach out to senior executives and product leaders to reach a consensus on the overall plan, scope of the change effort, and approach to execution.

In thinking about your agenda, you regard yourself as something of a revolutionary but with some developer tendencies.

As you introduce your idea, who will be on your side?

Tod Williams heads Spartan, which develops the best-selling utility billing software. Tod and most of his team joined Endo after their firm was bought out nine years ago. He thinks that one of the strengths of Endo is that the teams can operate with the spirit and enthusiasm of a start-up, while having the benefits of being part of a larger stable enterprise. Whenever the idea of centralization is brought up in rare crossteam meetings, Tod is the first one to tamp out that idea. He wants to keep the status quo but is willing to adjust when circumstances demand it. Tod is a traditionalist.

Rich Sanchez is Chief Operating Officer (COO) and has been with the company since the beginning. He started as a lowly IT consultant and gradually and patiently climbed the ranks. Rich recognizes that a large-scale overhaul is the best way to go. Endo could work loosely and still be effective when it had five product divisions, but the company is straining to operate nearly fifty autonomous units. Rich is a revolutionary.

Rochelle Burman is an external management consultant. You hired her to provide a third-party perspective. Her expertise is in helping companies to design structures that will improve organizational performance. She has told you more than once that the current model is inefficient, costly, and limits feedback. She isn't into change for the sake of change but thinks that the first step should be a comprehensive cost-benefit analysis of integrating key functions into headquarters. With a firm handle on the numbers, she thinks baby steps are the way to move forward. Rochelle is a developer.

Bernice Chang directs mergers and acquisitions, and she is in charge of identifying and acquiring new products. She started as a programmer, and joined M&A after business school. She is a big fan of Endo's entrepreneurial attitude, which she thinks is essential to keeping Endo ahead of the competition. While she doesn't want to see big changes, she is open to smaller adjustments that will streamline the organization. Bernice is an adjuster.

This cast of characters is presented only as an example. In a true scenario, there will be many stakeholders: customers, vendors, individual product teams, the VPs. While you ponder your idea, make a list and keep track of everyone who could be affected by your change effort.

You have the benefit of your past relationship with your colleagues. How have they reacted before to new ideas? Are they fine going along with small changes? Do they like to shake things up? In this case, you can see where your agenda is in alignment with the agendas of others. Rich is most closely aligned with your thinking, and you can see avenues where you could work with Rochelle and Bernice. With Rochelle, you have to appeal to her methodical numbers-based mindset. For Bernice, keep focused on the fact that the changes can be incremental, and stress that a streamlined organization will be more efficient. Tod, well, you will have to work on Tod. But you can ask for his input in coming up with mechanisms that will preserve the entrepreneurial nature of the product teams.

The point is that by having an understanding of how you view your initiative and how others view your initiative, you can begin to see what might motivate someone to join your change effort.

Expand Alliances

Now that you are mindful of the attitudes and approaches of others, you must map the political terrain. You must understand the agenda archetypes of others as they relate to your own. You need to:

Determine your agenda as it relates to your initiative. What is the scope of your change effort? Do you see yourself as a traditionalist, adjuster, developer, or revolutionary?

Identify the agenda of each stakeholder vis-à-vis the relevant issue. What are their long-term agendas?

Identify those who are like you, those who are in the opposite quadrant, and those who share either similar goals or similar implementation strategies.

By comparing your agenda archetype with that of others, you can begin to strategically anticipate allies and resistors, and potential allies and potential resistors. With this information, you can begin to seriously consider the people you should be spending time with and resources on to make sure they're in your corner. Campaigns fail because leaders try to mobilize everyone—or because they make overtures to the wrong group. Agenda movers appreciate that they need to be strategic in thinking about who they need on their side and selective in how they spend their campaign time and resources.

Staying with Your Base, Throwing a Hail-Mary Pass, and Playing the Middle

Allies are those who share your agenda, and it is easy for them to see where you're coming from. Because allies share your goals and approach, it is likely that they will join your campaign. To use political jargon, allies form your base. Allies agree with you on what you want to achieve and how you want to achieve it. They are at the core of your efforts to move your campaign forward. Allies provide your campaign with stability and consistency.

As in politics, having this small group of committed supporters is essential. Your challenge is to figure out how much of your limited time and resources to expend on them. Although allies are your core supporters, there's no guarantee they won't drift away—so you might need to make a concerted effort to keep your allies involved and engaged. How much of your precious time and resources do you want to spend on people who are already on your side?

Politicians sometimes fall into the trap of spending too much time with their base. On the face of it, playing to your base seems like a safe move. You will never build a broader coalition, however, if you focus your attention only on those who already agree with you. Unless your allies form an overwhelming majority, you won't be able to create change or get your innovations adopted with their support alone. To switch-up a metaphor, stay with your base too long and your beachhead could become a foxhole.

In the United States, many politicians have learned that staying

YOUR AGENDA ARCHETYPE	STAKEHOLDER'S AGENDA ARCHETYPE			
	Traditionalist	Adjuster	Developer	Revolutionary
Traditionalist	allies	potential allies	potential resistors	resistors
Adjuster	potential allies	allies	resistors	potential resistors
Developer	potential resistors	resistors	allies	potential allies
Revolutionary	resistors	potential resistors	potential allies	allies

with their base in early primary states may give them traction to receive their party's nomination for president. That said, the very concentrated effort they make early on may not translate into wide national support. The challenge is to know how to prevent your base from becoming the millstone around your neck.

Minimize, therefore, the effort you expend on your base. Do what you need to make sure they're in your corner, show them the appropriate respect, and keep them posted when you can, but don't spend your time covering the same ground over and over again.

What about resistors? Agenda movers accept that resistance is inevitable. They understand that leadership means sustaining campaigns in the face of resistance. As an agenda mover, you might feel that your challenge is to get those who do not think like you on your side. Your first instinct might be to spend a lot of time trying to win over resistors. You may reason that if you can convince those who most oppose you, everyone else will follow. However, deploying time and resources on those who are unlikely to come on board might not be an effective strategy.

As with their allies, agenda movers must weigh opposing concerns vis-à-vis resistors. You have to face the fact that resistors are unlikely to join you. You might, however, be able to keep them from working against you or sabotaging your efforts. Knowing who your resistors are and figuring out the nature of their resistance will help you decide how much time to spend with them.

Regardless of how much time and effort you decide to expend on resistors, it's important to know who they are and to be aware of the potential negative effect they can have on your agenda. In American football, the object is to score a touchdown by getting the ball into your opponent's end zone. Getting the ball down the field can sometimes be an interminable affair, but a player, in a desperate bid to speed up the scoring, may throw a Hail-Mary pass—a very long forward pass. Making a Hail-Mary pass is a risky proposition, in that its chances of success are low. If it works, the team scores a touchdown. If it doesn't work, the game could be lost. Similarly, if you make a Hail-Mary pass in an attempt to win over resistors, and they don't come around, the cost to you and your efforts to implement a new innovation or create change may be catastrophic.

Political leaders sometimes make a similar mistake when they convince themselves that their powers of persuasion are irresistible. With their unswerving belief in their own message, they conclude that if they just hang in a little longer, have just one more meeting, even the most entrenched resistor will see the light and come around. Politicians who make this mistake not only waste time and resources but also run the risk of weakening their base. By playing up to resistors, they risk alienating those who supported them in the first place.

Even more important than identifying allies and resistors is identifying potential allies and potential resistors. To win them over, you need to play the leadership game on the middle ground.

If you knew who was in your corner and who wasn't, there would be no need to be pragmatic. Agenda movers are leaders who understand that leading isn't about meeting jubilantly with allies or reasoning earnestly with resistors. Successful leaders understand that the real challenge is in the gray area—converting potential allies into allies and making sure that potential resistors are not transformed into full-fledged resistors.

Potential allies and potential resistors disagree with either your approach or your goals. Skillful negotiation may persuade these individuals to reconsider aspects of your agenda that differ from theirs. If you are not careful, potentials can easily switch to resistors. Potentials who share your goals but disagree with you on the approach might need a little push. You agree on where to go but want to take different routes to get there. Listen to their concerns, understand their approach, and be willing to compromise.

When dealing with potentials who share your approach but have a different sense of the bigger picture, your best bet is to use an attractive lure and hope they take the bait. Because your means are similar, you need to convince these individuals that your purpose is worth pursuing. If you successfully realign the divergent perspectives of potentials, you will establish a strong coalition of support.

The challenge in politics and in organizational life is to take the middle ground. Secure your base, make token gestures to resistors, but invest most of your effort in identifying and winning over your potential allies and potential resistors. This is where the leadership game is really played.

Why do change agendas stall in politics? Often, the fault lies with the intransigence of the two extremes. Change agendas are moved by debating the nuances of goals and approaches—not compromising overall ideologies—and by making microadjustments tailored to potential allies and potential resistors. Some adjustments will be aimed at individuals who essentially agree with you, at least in the main, but who have concerns that they feel are too important to ignore (i.e., potential allies). Other modifications to your agenda will target those who might object to your agenda but not so fully that they can't be pacified with small concessions (i.e., potential resistors). If you can negotiate these microadjustments successfully, you are on your way to building a strong coalition of support.

Agenda movers understand that they must spend much of their efforts pulling in potential allies and mollifying potential resistors. They can learn one lesson from politicians. Those who run successful campaigns are strategic in where they focus their efforts. They don't try to dance with all the parties. They are well aware that their resources are limited and their time precious, and they know they've got to be smart about how to spend them. The same is true in an organization. As an agenda mover, you will analyze the goals and agendas of other stakeholders and use this information to strategically design your campaign.

Expect the "Yes-But" Game

As a pragmatic agenda mover, you realize the importance of understanding where others are coming from. You have a sense of your resistors and potential resistors, and your allies and potential allies. Now you have to anticipate their specific criticisms. Even those who think like you, your allies, will have questions, inquire about details, and ask for specifics. This is the positive nature of organizational checks and balances. Just because marketing has an idea doesn't mean research and development has to accept it. Just because a Democratic president has an idea doesn't mean the Democrats in

Congress should pass it. Specific criticisms must be dealt with if you want to create change.

Aristotle famously said, "Criticism is something we can avoid easily by saying nothing, doing nothing, and being nothing." Without disrespect to Aristotle, avoiding action isn't necessarily a guard against criticism. In fact, you will be criticized for not taking action. Criticism is one of the realities of leadership, and there is nothing to do but accept it. Instead of letting critics take you by surprise, learn to anticipate and respond to criticism without losing your head.

If one thing keeps leaders up at night, it's criticism. In organizational life, no matter how well prepared you are, how carefully you've laid out your plans, how elegantly you crunched the numbers, there is always someone ready and willing to find the hole, pick up on that point you didn't fully explain, and question your intentions.

When pragmatic leaders do their preparatory homework, they don't focus on the content of their initiative or bask in the brilliance of their idea. Rather, they try to predict the arguments that others will make. To better anticipate what challenges and objections others will have, pragmatic leaders put themselves into the shoes of others.

Some criticism will be in the form of direct confrontation. Your ideas will be attacked head-on. This is the bare-knuckled "got-you" game—the well-placed punch that can bring down your change agenda. However, there is a more subtle—and just as damaging—approach that critics can use to challenge your ideas. This is the "yes-but" game—the same criticism but framed in a positive tone.

The brutal "got-you" game is not played as often as the softer "yes-but" game. When someone challenges you, they won't denounce your idea blatantly, but they might say something like, "Yes, I can see what you mean, but . . . " Or "Yes, of course we need to do something, but I find this part of your idea to be troubling." These criticisms are not benign simply because they are delivered with a smile. They can still derail your change effort.

You can win the "yes-but" game by anticipating seven possible criticisms:

1. Your Idea Is Too Risky

As soon as you present a new proposal, someone will suggest that your idea will put the organization in danger, threatening its highly valued accomplishments and successes. They prefer the well-traveled road of safety. Your idea has an uncertain outcome. Not only that, it is expensive, too.

You have to be careful with the people who make this argument, because they won't tell you at first. They will ask you questions, and you will think that they are genuinely interested in your initiative. Just as you are about to leave, they tell you, in dulcet, reassuring tones, "You know, this idea is a bit risky." With just a few words, they can puncture your enthusiasm.

Whenever you propose a new idea, others will invariably point out its risks. No matter how golden your idea, how honorable your intent, how pure your ambition, others will maintain that your idea has the potential to cause, at worst, catastrophe, and at best, a major setback. When others proclaim that your idea is too risky, they are trying to freeze further action.

Be aware that some people regard all change with suspicion. With the your-idea-is-too-risky crowd, the risk is never worth the potential gain. There is always too much to lose.

2. Your Idea Will Make Things Worse

Another argument you will hear in the early stages of your initiative is that your idea will result in the exact opposite of its intended outcome. They may laugh and give you a slap on the shoulder as they say, "It's going to boomerang, and if you think things are bad now, that idea of yours is going to turn things upside down."

The beauty of this argument is that your detractors will say it straight out. They won't beat around the bush or make some effort at pretending they are on your side. Their confidence and self-assurance may be unnerving. If you stick around, they will paint a dreary doomsday scenario where all the troubles of the world will fall on your shoulders and be your fault.

Resistors often make the argument that your idea will make things worse. They'll say that while the idea on the surface seems fine, down the line something is certain to go wrong. They will claim they've seen many organizational change initiatives come and go, and learned the hard way that messing with the system always backfires. In the spy trade, this is called blowback.

3. Your Idea Won't Change a Thing

Another time-tested argument used to undermine agenda movers is to claim that their efforts won't change a thing. They will be exceedingly kind, like an elderly relative patting a child on the head. Then they will say that they are sorry, but given the organization's history, no matter how wonderful your idea, you don't have a snowball's chance in a hot oven to succeed.

Of course they are rooting for you. They may tell you that they were young, once, too, and had ideas that were going to set the world on fire, until the cold water of reality extinguished the flame. Listen, they are trying to save you a lot of time and futile effort. If you think about it, they'll say, they are doing you a favor.

Much debate in the political arena centers on this type of resistance. Developers and adjusters may want to move an idea ahead while revolutionaries may counter that the idea at hand will change nothing. Think of the debate over banking regulation in the wake of 2008 financial crisis and the passage of the Dodd-Frank bill, which was meant to correct the financial environment and protect the economy from future crisis. One of the critiques of Dodd-Frank is that it would fundamentally keep the status quo. When faced with such an argument, you have to ground your apparent incrementalism in very specific examples and show that while the idea might not change everything it will change something.

4. You Don't Know the Issues Well Enough

They may disagree on the objectives of your initiative or take issue with how you've cast the issues. They'll say things like, "Well, you did a lot of work thinking about issue Y, but issue Z is the real problem. You have to deal with that first." Or your resistors may challenge you on the details: "You should have known that the learning curve for that new finance software was going to be steep. If you were more familiar with the staff, you never would have ordered it." Or, "You haven't been here long enough to know about the marketing strategy in the Midwest to start changing policy."

There isn't just one center in today's organizations; there isn't one nexus from where ideas are sanctioned to emerge. There isn't just one expert who is qualified to lead a given initiative. In today's organizations, ideas can and do come from anywhere, and the people taking the lead aren't always the ones with the most expertise or the deepest experience—but they have the freedom to rely on those with expertise and experience to guide them through the shoals of innovation.

New hires and employees in lower ranks of the organization are notoriously susceptible to the charge of not knowing the issues well enough. Suppose you're a new HR director in a large retail organization. You're asked to write an analysis of the chain's compensation structure and make recommendations. You go ahead and draw up a plan, drawing on data from the industry and your experience in the field. Inevitably, employees who will lose out if your recommendations are adopted will complain that your report is groundless—that you're too new, you just don't understand "how things work around here."

The main goal of this argument is to denounce you as leader of the initiative and to publicly question your credibility and legitimacy. The condescending tone taken by your critics implies that you haven't done your homework. Your critics will say that you don't understand the larger context, that you don't have enough information, that you lack sufficient experience with the organization. The danger of this argument is its outward legitimacy. If there is a ring of truth to what your critics are saying, your initiative is likely to be derailed.

5. You're Doing It Wrong

"We agreed on the direction we wanted for the company, but we had differences of opinion on how to get there." You've probably heard a variant of this phrase before, especially in the context a news-making interview with an insider on the exit of a chief executive. Translated from business-speak, what the source is telling the reporter is: "The CEO was doing it wrong."

Organizations get set in their ways, and there is usually a preferred procedure for accomplishing basic tasks. Sometimes "the way it's always been done" works well for routine administrative tasks. When you're implementing new ideas and taking the organization in fresh directions—which some people may find discomfiting—then you are going to hear that you're doing it wrong. Your critics will appear to be sympathetic to your intention, but their assessment of how you're going about it will be antagonistic.

Suppose you have to decide what to do with an unprofitable, and somewhat remote, unit of your organization. The numbers don't add up, and the upkeep of the extra office space is costing the organization money. After consultation with other stakeholders, you make a decision: the remote office will be closed in six months, and in the meantime, you'll make plans to absorb as much of its staff as possible into the main operation. Immediately, the complaints start coming. People will say six months is too soon; the closure should be phased in over a period of years. Or six months is too long: why drag out the inevitable? Or the office shouldn't be closed at all, but reorganized.

Like the you-don't-know-the-issues-well-enough argument, the you're-doing-it-wrong argument doesn't offer specific criticism directed at aspects of your idea. Instead, these arguments aim to overturn your effort by attacking you as a person. Often, this strategy is employed when the leader has a notable weakness or other vulnerability. By focusing on your lack of technical expertise or your inexperience, skeptics aim to raise questions in the minds of others about your ability to lead the effort.

This argument of resistance doesn't depend on the relative merits or demerits of your idea. Rather, it attacks your ability to execute. Maybe there was nothing wrong with your idea to improve the accounting system, but how you implemented the system is open to criticism. The you're-doing-it-wrong crowd doesn't explicitly oppose your idea, but they actively work to sideline your idea by attacking your ability to lead.

6. It's Been Done Before

For an organizational newcomer, this argument can be deadly. You weren't around the first time that a new compensation system was introduced—and failed miserably. You weren't there when the organization's last efforts at centralization resulted in more fragmentation and new silos. "We've been there, done that, and bought the T-shirt," the old-timers will say when you unveil your proposal.

When you launch your initiative, you are going to hear, "We tried this before and it didn't work—so why try now?" This sort of resistance is predicated on the assumption that there is historical knowledge or past experience that makes your agenda irrelevant or doomed to failure. Senior staff members, the keepers of institutional memory, often make this case.

This challenge, in most cases, is straightforward to take on. More often than not, when people resist your agenda with "it's been done before" they are speaking in generalities. Institutional history, organizational memory, and recollections of past practice are remembered in generalities, not in concrete empirical terms. Your resistors could be generally correct, but they could miss the specifics of past practices and fail to realize how your suggestion is nuanced differently.

Whether the objection is a knee-jerk reaction or is rooted in honest feedback, it is important for you to be prepared. To face the objection you need to specifically compare past practice and policy to your intended agenda. The best way to burst the balloon of generalities is with the needle of empirical reality.

7. You Have Ulterior Motives

The definitive case that can be made against you is that you are doing this for your own sinister reasons. The only reason you are pushing your agenda is because you—or your allies—will personally reap some untold reward. While you think that your agenda serves the greater good and helps the organization, skeptics and resistors will doubt your virtue and explain away your motivation in terms of self-interest.

Whenever you try to move an agenda in an organization, others may mistrust the idea or the initiative. Ideas are never entirely untainted, and it is too easy for others to think that by proposing the idea that you are looking out for number one.

You've had this feeling yourself. You might question why someone is doing something—to make a good impression on the boss? Do they have a hidden agenda? What is their core intention? By the same token, others may similarly question your motives and intent.

The reality is that pure altruism is not part of the day-to-day organizational reality. Organizational behavior is such that you will be unlikely to do anything that is blatantly against your interests and those of your supporters. Therefore, in the context of this simple reality, the critique that you are self-serving can always be made. Obviously, you will rarely be altruistic, and will never be, if you can help it, self-destructive. That is not to say that you do not have the collective good in mind.

There is a tendency in the contemporary organizational world to be distrustful, and that's not necessarily bad. Questioning motives is just another form of checks and balances. Your challenge is to not overreact. Instead, take the time to anticipate the types of motivational challenges that others will make.

▲ ▲ ▲

Agenda movers understand how to react to yes-but arguments. They accept the inevitably of yes-but challenges as part of their campaign.

In dealing with "yes-but" arguments, weigh your reaction. The most severe test of your pragmatic leadership is how you react to criticism. You may prefer direct confrontation, charging the other party with making false or inaccurate claims. You may try to delegitimize your challengers by bringing their untenable positions to light. You may choose to try to skirt around your challengers, finding support elsewhere and minimizing the need to engage them directly. Whichever route you choose, you need to be able to absorb their blows, respond to their comments, and if they make some good points—incorporate what they say into your strategy.

Don't let a well-delivered barb deflate your confidence. Don't allow yourself to get involved in an escalating competition of egos. Letting criticism get personal will blur your objectivity, absorb your time and energy, and make others think that your ego is more important to you than seeing your idea come to fruition. Getting involved in a competition of egos can easily get you thrown out of the game.

Consider a research institute that depends on external funding. The funding will sustain the immediate work of the lab, while providing some infrastructure support for the institute as a whole. A lead researcher can benefit from landing larger grants, but is open to criticism that they are out for their own interests. What is lost is the understanding that by securing a grant—the researcher's interests are provided for, but so are the interests of the institution.

While there is a distinction between individual motives and collective motives, the twain do meet. Don't shy away from having your own motives to create change, but make sure that others know that your plan will also satisfy the needs of the collective.

Anticipating the "yes-but" and the more aggressive "got-you" games is essential, but you have to guard against becoming suspicious and paranoid. Agenda movers know that preparing for different types of criticism helps them to improve their ideas. By anticipating the seven arguments of resistance, you will be able to enhance the appeal of your initiative—that is, if you can address their legitimate concerns early in the process, you have a better chance of pulling them onboard.

▲　▲　▲

Anticipating where others are coming from, understanding the political terrain, and categorizing the agendas of others are skills honed
by the best agenda movers. They do their homework before they go
into the meeting. They map the power players, try to understand
the political mind-set of others, and try to unravel the agendas of
others. Then they engage in a mind exercise, trying to predict the
arguments they might encounter as they move their new innovation
or effort of change forward.

You often hear about doing your homework before charging full-
steam ahead. These methodical, reflective exercises anticipate the
reaction of others once you launch an idea. They are essential drills
you must practice.

But you have to remember one thing above all. Once you suggest
an idea there is no taking it back. Once you propose a change or hint
at a new direction the genie is out of the bottle. If you didn't anticipate the reaction of others, chaos may follow. It is imperative that
you do your homework.

3

MOBILIZE YOUR CAMPAIGN

Get Initial Support

MOBILIZE

You've put your skills of anticipation to good use. You've mapped the key stakeholders. You know who the Top Dogs, Gatekeepers, Gurus, and Players are. You've deciphered the nuances of power—that is, you've figured out who has authority and who has influence. You've been able to determine the goals and approaches of others, and you are mindful of their agendas. You've become sensitive to your allies and resistors. You've prepared for the seven arguments of resistance that you're likely to hear. You've done your pragmatic homework.

Now you have to get initial support. Unlike anticipation, mobilization is no longer a question of homework or an exercise you do in your head or work out on paper. You have to get into a coalition mind-set. You have to introduce your idea to a core of individuals who will rally around it with some sense of cohesion, purpose, and intent. You have to share your ideas with others to ensure that you're moving in the right direction.

To mobilize others you must: focus your message; justify your agenda; establish your credibility; and gauge your support.

Focus Your Message

Focusing a lens causes light rays from the subject to converge on a central point. A photographer can choose to focus on different parts of his subject, depending on his audience and the image he wants to produce.

Focusing your message means making sure your message is clear, unambiguous, and suited to your audience. Sometimes, choosing your audience is the first step in focusing your message. Make sure you're introducing your idea at the right time, in the right way, and to the right people.

Think of Woodrow Wilson and his failed efforts to get Americans to support the League of Nations after World War I. The United States was entering an isolationist phase, and the American people were not ready to join a global effort. Wilson couldn't do much about the timing; he was going to be president only until 1921. But as described earlier in this book, Wilson may have succeeded despite the bad timing if he had not made two big mistakes. First, Wilson chose his audience poorly. He tried to get his message out to the American public writ large, rather than winning over key stakeholders. Second, having chosen his audience, Wilson failed to tailor his message to them. Rather than focusing on the proposed League's practical implications, Wilson emphasized its broad, lofty goals. In doing so, he unwittingly created a wall of resistance.

Let's consider now a different example. In the summer of 1862, in the second year of the American Civil War, the issue of emancipation was hotly contested in the Union. Sentiment was divided over questions such as compensation (should Southern slave owners be compensated for the loss of their "property," and by how much?) and the extent of emancipation (should slaves be freed only in the rebel Confederate states or also in the slave-owning border states—Kentucky, Missouri, Maryland, Delaware, and West Virginia—which had remained in the Union?). Abraham Lincoln's own views were that slavery was abhorrent, but he understood the political and social delicacy of the issue. He felt that emancipation, however, would give the Union a strong moral mission to rally behind and would help the war effort by facilitating the recruitment of blacks into the Union Army.

Lincoln resolved to push for a gradual and compensated emancipation. When that effort failed to take off, he was determined to use his authority as commander-in-chief under the War Powers Act to immediately emancipate all the slaves in Confederate territory. Slaves in Union territory could be emancipated only by the state governments or by an act of Congress, a process completed with passage of the Thirteenth Amendment in 1865. In September 1862, Lincoln announced that he would order the emancipation of all slaves in Confederate states that did not return to the Union by January 1, 1863. On the appointed day, he issued the formal Emancipation Proclamation that declared that any slave living in the ten Confederate states not under Union control would be "forever free."

Lincoln hated slavery, and wrote that "if slavery is not wrong, nothing is wrong."[1] But he knew that he was likely to fail if he tried to end slavery without preparing the ground. The outcome of the Civil War was by no means certain, and he knew that without the support of the slave-owning border states and other political actors who opposed secession but not slavery, all could be lost. Lincoln waited until he had been in office nearly two years before he made his move. He took the time to establish his credibility, to build support among the public (through an open letter published in an abolitionist newspaper), and to consult with key political figures, including members of his cabinet and governors of the Union states.

The Emancipation Proclamation was a document of restraint. It was silent on the fate of the nearly one million slaves who lived in Union-held territories at the time of its issue. By careful crafting of the document, Lincoln was able to generate the maximum amount of support at a crucial period in the war. He was able to find a way to start the country on the rocky path toward Reconstruction.

Lincoln succeeded where Wilson failed because he focused his message. Specifically, he did three things. First, Lincoln timed his move well. Second, he found a common language that he could use when communicating with his potential and likely supporters. And third, he targeted his audience with care.

Control the Timing (If You Can)

While leaders may be constantly in campaign mode, thinking about how to get things done, there is a difference between private discussions about an issue and a public campaign. A public campaign means that you are committed to a specific direction. It means that you have put your intentions on the table and make it clear to others what you want to accomplish.

Selecting the timing for publicly launching the campaign is important, but it is even more important to make sure your idea is fully thought through before you say anything. Once you make the announcement, there is no backing down. You can't hold up your hands in the face of resistance and say you were joking.

Don't bring your ideas to the table until they are cooked, especially if you're not sure whether your idea is something you're going to pursue. A surefire way to ruin your credibility is to be labeled as someone who doesn't follow through. At the same time, don't wait too long before announcing your idea, or you may miss a crucial window of opportunity. In this regard, consulting with others can be very helpful in determining when the timing is right to announce your plan. Don't hold your initiative too close to the vest, but solicit advice or evaluations from a few people you trust.

Perfectionism is one of your chief enemies here. This is especially true in areas such as product development. While you're working to perfect your prototype, your competitor might already be preparing to go to market. Think your idea through fully, be certain that you are ready to launch your campaign—but don't keep waiting for the ideal time. There may never be one.

Consider a CEO. Everything was running more or less smoothly, but she felt the need to "do something" with her tenure that would ensure that the company would be on solid financial footing into the future. With much pomp and circumstance, it was announced that there would a new budget model and a new allocation of internal resources. Although the plan was supposed to be announced at some later date, details of the plan emerged, and the C-suite started to feel some pushback from units that were potentially affected by the changes. Instead of unveiling the new model and getting on top of the messaging, the launch was delayed while the finance team went in to do more tweaks that would placate the early dissenters. Once again a date was targeted, but the same scenario played out again, with different players. The launch was delayed while adjustments were made to the plan. This happened a third time, and ultimately, the new budget model was presented to the entire organization— and landed with a thud.

To the CEO's surprise, not everyone was onboard. Because of the long, drawn-out process, the resistors had time to grow in number and were ready to attack. Her decision to delay and try to marshal as much support as she could backfired, and she ended up with a weak initiative that didn't have the core of support that she needed to sustain it. The CEO was moved out, and the budget model walked back soon after.

If you are already in a leadership position, and if you introduce new ideas often, you are used to setting timelines and deadlines. Adhering to your deadlines becomes more important as you climb the organizational or political ladder. If you make it a practice to postpone crucial deadlines, others will question not only your idea but also your ability to follow through. The lesson is that missing deadlines, even for good reason, can be detrimental to both your campaign and your credibility. It's important that you don't make it a practice to miss deadlines.

Find a Common Language

An idea can be stymied after the initial proposal because the person initiating the idea fails to tailor the message to the other party. If you're not getting your message across, you might not be talking on the same level as the person whose support you are seeking. Your vocabulary—and your promises—may be too grand. Or your vocabulary may be so concrete and specific that the other party misses the nuances of your proposal. In both cases, the consequence is that the situation becomes one of talking past each other. Even though both parties may have some common intention, how you frame the conversation will have an impact on how you move your agenda.

Some may view your proposal as being broad and ideological and too focused on big strategic goals. Others may consider your idea as being too specific and excessively focused on the exact steps of how your coalition is going to make things happen.

Consider the tensions in peace politics of the Palestinian-Israeli conflict. It seems that everyone cannot agree on the definition of "peace." One faction may have a concrete notion of peace that encompasses the exchanging of ambassadors and sharing in economic and cultural activities. Other groups see peace as basically "live and let live"—a cold peace. One of the challenges that a peace-agenda mover could have is to build a coalition composed of parties with inconsistent notions of peace. However, initially establishing consensus around a broad notion of peace may be difficult. Instead the agenda mover might find it easier to focus the dialogue on nuts-and-bolts issues. The emphasis on the details might establish a concrete focus that may, at a different point, allow for more normative or ideological consensus.

Rather than being caught in the continuous debate over the broad issue of peace, if Israeli and Palestinian leaders could negotiate the details of a shared industrial zone, this could possibly be the first step toward a common notion of peace. Broad strategic consensus can emerge from a nuts-and-bolts discussion.

The ideal for the agenda mover is to persuade others to join the coalition by dealing with broad strategic issues first and then work out the nuts-and-bolts details. It may be the case that while you talk about broad strategic issues, your colleagues want to discuss fundamentals. When both sides are coming from different places, everyone talks past each other. Never was this better exemplified than during the 1978 Camp David Summit when Jimmy Carter brought Israeli prime minister Menachem Begin and Egyptian president Anwar Sadat together to move Carter's peace agenda. The problem was that the Egyptian leader was idealistic and flamboyant and spoke in broad principled terms while the Israeli prime minister was analytical and understood issues in tactical concrete terms. Sadat was comfortable leaving the details to others while Begin wanted to get to the microminutia of the details. Begin wanted to move incrementally and specify every detail—which Sadat saw as a stalling tactic.

As Jimmy Carter quickly learned at Camp David, however, when there isn't agreement on the broad issues at the outset, a better strategy is to go in through the back door. That is, to begin the dialogue addressing specific nuts-and-bolts issues. If you want your coalition to have the support of people who strategically object to your position, you are going to have to work out some key details collaboratively. A small degree of agreement will allow everyone to achieve a level of trust and understanding that can lead to a broad strategic consensus. An agenda mover understands that chipping away at issues can be a means of moving the campaign ahead—that agreement on broader issues can emerge from nuts-and-bolts discussions.

Normative messages can be broad, enveloping—and impossible to disagree with. Who would argue against peace? The trouble is, normative messages leave too much room for interpretation. While normative messages may cast a wide net, thus seeming to broaden your support base, once people begin to think about what you've actually said, you may lose them.

This is the problem you will face if you initiate change without delineating the details. While you might feel you're playing it smart by putting out a broad message that includes everyone, soon enough someone will ask, "Where's the beef?" But if you make the message too concrete, they'll ask, "Where's the griddle?"

You can give your change effort definition and boundaries by specifying key details, delineating what needs to be done, and breaking broad concepts into specific steps. With a message that addresses specifics, everyone knows exactly where you want to go and what you want to do. Remember to put your idea into its larger context. Your listeners need to know both what you plan to do, and why.

As an agenda mover, balance your vision with specifics. As you delve into specific issues, you'll develop opportunities for compromise. That is the premier pragmatic lesson of coalition politics: If you want people to join your campaign, find a common language.

Target Your Initial Audience
You can introduce your idea to a few select leaders who you think can help you create a coalition. Or you can go straight to the public

(if you're a politician) or to the group or organization as a whole, with the intention of creating a wave effect.

Both strategies have advantages and disadvantages. Speaking to select leaders might boomerang if you're seen as engaging in an elite conspiracy. Going straight to the public means you might have to dilute your idea so it will appeal to everyone. Politicians sometimes face this dilemma. Focus on a handful of political leaders and hope they have the clout to move the idea ahead? Or start with a wide constituency—use the bully pulpit, as it were—with the hope of sweeping the bosses into the coalition with a groundswell of support? The two options are not mutually exclusive. But sometimes, one strategy is more appropriate than the other.

Group momentum can sour if your audience includes a large number of resistors and potential resistors. A few heckles from the crowd may give way to a mob mentality. This was what happened when congressmen from conservative Southern states held town hall meetings to rally support for president Barack Obama's health care agenda during the summer of 2010. The forums attracted hostile audiences, and some gatherings ended in physical violence. When launching your idea with resistors and potential resistors, avoid the crowd and connect with key stakeholders on an individual basis.

The advantages of launching your ideas to key individuals are obvious. You can address their personal, subjective concerns. There is no crowd pressure, and it is easier for you to diffuse possible tension. Approaching individuals is an effective strategy when you know you're going to have to deal with resistors and potential resistors. Even if they oppose your goals and approach, they may grant you a meeting out of courtesy or because they genuinely want to understand where you're coming from. If you meet with a resistor, show how your agenda serves the best interests of the organization.

There's no right or wrong answer. The lesson to remember is to be thoughtful about whom you're turning to for initial support. Knowing your likely audience will help keep you from over- or under-reaching. If you've mapped the stakeholders in your group or organization, you'll have a sense of whom you want to target first.

Justify Your Agenda

You know there is a need for action. You have to get others to go along with you to make your idea a reality. How do you sell your idea? What do you tell your allies? Do you shape a different pitch for resistors? What about your potentials? How do you frame your idea in a way that makes them want to come on board?

Even if you're the Top Dog in the organization, as an agenda mover you won't want to take a hierarchical, top-down approach. This is likely to lead only to conflict, blame, and resentment down the road. Instead, you need to justify your idea. There are four types of arguments you can call upon to do this.

"Look at the Numbers"

When you're trying to justify an initiative, looking at the numbers is always a good idea. Doing a cost-benefit analysis and a developing a well-structured presentation of alternatives shows that your effort is backed up by real research and an understanding of what's happening in your organization and in the relevant industry or sector. Quantification, statistics, and models are hard to argue with. This is the primary type of argument used to justify actions in all sectors of the economy. This is how young MBAs are kept fully employed.

A rational argument—"look at the numbers"—presents a logical justification for change. A careful cost-benefit analysis, where costs and benefits are demonstrated and quantified, provides a sound reason for taking action. Your argument will emphasize the empirical payoff of your agenda.

You may be most successful in using a rational argument to call for action in organizations with a strong planning culture, where rigorous quantitative analysis is required before any decision is made. A rational justification may work less well in mission-driven organizations, where qualitative factors have a wider berth. The rational argument may falter in highly changeable situations where projections of future costs and benefits are difficult to quantify with any degree of accuracy—such as any initiative that relies on a forecast of the company's future stock price. Additionally, certain costs might not be significant in dollar terms but are strategically important. In highly volatile times, a rational argument is much less persuasive.

In the last quarter century, quantification has dominated the business vocabulary. You live in a world of model building and statistics, where components are broken down into matrices, impact and payoff are analyzed with regression, and everything is reduced to a mind-set of cost-benefit and return on investment.

Even when you know that data is fallible, statistics vulnerable, and models inconclusive, there is a degree of comfort by having a stack of numbers behind you as ammunition for getting support for your agenda. That said, in a world of probability and chance, agenda movers don't put all their eggs in the rational argument basket. They know that numbers don't tell the whole story. Sometimes agenda movers look to their neighbors for ideas and think, "If they can do it, why can't we?"

"Everyone Is Doing It"

While the rational argument relies on data and logic, the mimicry argument derives its legitimacy from the fact that other organizations have successfully implemented a similar initiative. Think of "best practices." The mimicry argument is often used when an organization lacks the time, resources, or data to pursue an alternative solution.

While imitation may be the sincerest form of flattery, imitation can also be a viable business justification strategy. Leaders often use the mimicry argument as a heuristic to illustrate the benefits of a potential initiative. The mimicry technique often masks the rationalization process.

Higher education is not immune from the pressures of the mimicry argument. In 2006, Harvard discontinued its early admissions program as a means of improving financial aid opportunities for students from families with lower incomes. Two weeks later, Princeton followed suit, citing a desire to simplify the admissions process. Naturally, Princeton was playing follow-the-leader with Harvard. One week later, the University of Virginia eliminated its early admissions program, and later the University of Florida and other universities did the same.

In 2011, the pendulum swung in the other direction. First, the University of Virginia reinstated its early admissions program but with a difference—this time, early decisions would be nonbinding. Taking their cue from Virginia, Harvard and Princeton resumed offering prospective students early admissions options. The consensus seemed to be that the abolition of early decisions left the elite schools at a disadvantage when recruiting top students from lower income families.

The mimicry argument works best in larger organizations with a planning orientation. Larger organizations often feel an affiliation with their peer companies and like to "stick with the herd." The mimicry argument works less well in small companies that value creativity and innovation. In any type of organization, the mimicry argument is problematic when organizations adopt change by blindly copying others, without considering the appropriateness of a change initiative for their organization.

Both cost-benefit analysis and best practices have their limitations. So agenda movers may have to resort to the pressure argument: "They're making us do it."

"They're Making Us Do It"

In trying to get initial support, sometimes an agenda mover will maintain a sense that there is no choice. The pressure is such that the action must be taken. There is a sense that someone or something is making us do it. Market pressures—the competition might simply be so fierce and heavy that simple survival necessitates it. These pressures may be such that one cannot even think of lagging behind. IBM's initial commitment to the mainframe over the laptop eventually became impossible to maintain because market pressures soon forced the company to take action.

There's also the omnipotence of politics and regulations. Sometimes federal regulations and local ordinances require organizations to change their processes or how they do business. Such a scenario offers a strong third-party justification for change. If the law or other regulation forces you to change your practice, then you have to change your practice. No one can blame or question you for the change if you have no choice. Fortunately or unfortunately, in social change this type of regulatory activity is often necessary to give an agenda mover the tipping point argument. Sure, there might be some pressure from the outside, but sometimes it takes that extra-regulatory visible public pressure to get someone to act. This is especially true if this is on behalf of a collective good whose benefit is not obvious.

Think about the strategic decisions that investment banks had to make following regulatory reform after the 2008 financial crisis. Specifically, the Frank-Dodd bill prohibited banks from proprietary trading, or betting on the markets with the firm's own money. In firms like Goldman Sachs, JPMorgan, Morgan Stanley, and Citigroup, proprietary trading had the highest margins and was a real profit driver (and also the cause of a great deal of trouble). These firms' chief compliance and risk officers knew what they had to say to the hotshot trading chiefs. It was something like, "I know you guys don't want to close down the highest-grossing business in the firm, and we hoped we wouldn't have to do it either. But we have no choice—they're making us do it!"

Suppose the numbers don't quite work, the best practices aren't there, and no one is holding a gun to your head. You may have to try the moral-emotional appeal—the people-expect-it-of-us argument.

"People Expect It of Us"

When using a standards argument, you make your case on the basis of the high expectations of the larger community. This argument holds that it's better in the long term to do the right thing, even if there could be a short-term dent in the bottom line. The payoff will be greater customer loyalty or more community trust.

Google decided to pull out of China in 2010 in response to the Chinese government's insistence that it would monitor Google China's search-engine traffic and censor specific content, such as references to the suppression of the 1989 Tiananmen Square protests. Google's cofounders Larry Page and Sergey Brin opposed government interference, and in January 2010, Google dropped all content filters, which allowed Chinese users unfettered access to all that the internet had to offer. The Chinese government blocked all access to Google in China and asked the company to leave the country.

Google had a lot to lose by leaving. China had the largest number of internet users in the world, and Google had invested significantly in the country. Page and Brin argued that leaving China was as much a business decision as a moral one. They made the claim that people expected Google to act differently than other tech companies such as Yahoo! or Microsoft (neither had qualms about acquiescing to censorship demands). They felt it was Google's responsibility to represent accessibility and freedom of information. Furthermore, compliance with the Chinese government would irreparably damage Google's reputation. Pulling out of China—despite heavy financial losses—was both the right and the smart thing to do.

Citing the moral high ground is a risky approach to selling your idea. Your stakeholders may see things differently than you do, and may not appreciate your advocacy. But your customers, clients, and community may be very responsive to a decision to do the right thing. It is difficult for someone to challenge your agenda if everyone agrees it is the moral course of action.

▲ ▲ ▲

There are four kinds of arguments that you can draw on to get people initially behind your ideas—the numbers are on your side, others are doing it, outside pressures are forcing your hand, and there is a moral case for taking action. The challenge for an agenda mover, in trying to get initial support, is to wisely balance the four arguments to counter different forms of opposition and appeal to different members of your audience. With experience, agenda movers become adept at incorporating the four types of arguments to strengthen the case for change.

In trying to mobilize initial support for his health care agenda, President Obama used the four types of arguments in turn—and each time, he found himself stymied by his opponents. When he said his health care initiative would reduce costs, he became tangled in spreadsheets and Congressional Budget Office reports. When he made the case that in moving to universal health care the United States would be following best practice, his critics accused him of making false comparisons among nations. When he insisted that the initiative was really a response to forces beyond his control, he faced delay tactics. When he tried to make a moral argument that access to health care was a right, not a privilege, he was thwarted with constitutional arguments.

Obama made progress only when he advanced his initiative on all four fronts. As an agenda mover, be agile in presenting your case, and use all the arguments at your disposal. Detail the costs and benefits, define the comparisons, illustrate the pressures, and lay out the moral expectations. Don't be passive when persuading others.

Establish Credibility

You've convinced them there's a need to take action. Now you have to convince them you can deliver. You have to demonstrate that you understand the issues inside and out and that you're sensitive to internal concerns and pressures. You need to show that you have the capacity and willingness to go the distance.

As an agenda mover, you have to be credible. Others have to believe that you can get the job done. You can't just say, "Hey, I'm the guy for the job." You have to be smart and establish your expertise, show that the opportunity for action is available, lean on your positional authority, and demonstrate your integrity. If you fire on these four cylinders, others will have no problem believing that you can deliver.

"I Know What I'm Talking About"
One way to get others to back your agenda is to show them you know what you're talking about. This is not a game of modesty, although

you have to avoid outward arrogance. Let them know that you have the knowledge necessary to validate and affirm the legitimacy of your change effort or new innovation.

Ask yourself how you obtained the knowledge that makes you an expert. To answer this question, you need to reflect on the value of your expertise. You have to communicate to others that your specialized knowledge makes your involvement essential to the successful completion of your campaign.

Coming out of the Revolutionary War, the fledgling states of the new American nation were riddled with debt and on the verge of default. The new nation needed to create a centralized system to guarantee the country's debts, and yet the states felt that they should be in control. President George Washington called on Alexander Hamilton to transform the money supply in order to bring the country back from default and restore confidence in the economy. In response, Hamilton created the U.S. Treasury bond—but his plan ran into stiff resistance from Congress. To convince Washington that he had the right plan and was the right person to carry it out, Hamilton read almost every available text on economics and constructed an accurate balance sheet, showing how much each state and agency owed. Washington was persuaded by the gravity of the problem and by Hamilton's raw technical ability. Washington threw his political might behind the younger, less popular Hamilton and prevented the country from defaulting on its obligations.

The efforts of Spencer Cox and Mark Harrington, members of the Act Up movement and the Treatment Action Group, illustrate the idea that sometimes showing others that you possess specialized knowledge is the only way to get them to listen to you. Cox and Harrington became involved in the AIDS movement as protestors with the Act Up effort, but it was their decision to study the science of AIDS, pharmaceutical industry, and the government funding and drug approval process that enabled them to influence federal legislation regarding the AIDS research effort and expose inadequate clinical trials, ultimately influencing the development of an effective antiretroviral drug.[2] It was Cox and Harrington's ability to understand the facts and data of a complicated disease that implored others to act.[3]

Like Hamilton, your challenge is to convey your expertise to others. Your expertise may have multiple dimensions, and it is essential that others know the full range of your knowledge. This leads to a common problem people face when trying to convey their expertise: arrogance.

You may have the technical expertise and training to understand particularly sophisticated aspects of a problem. You may have political expertise from your experience in your organization or community and understand the systemic obstacles to change. You must assert yourself as an expert who is uniquely qualified to push an agenda forward. But it's important to tread this line carefully. You don't want others to reject your idea simply because they perceive you as self-involved and arrogant.

Think of the young computer programmer or the new market analyst with a briefcase full of esoteric econometric models. Expertise is sometimes conveyed with a dash of self-importance, even if unintentional. When telling someone something they don't know, do so in a reflective manner. Don't be authoritarian or a know-it-all. Suggest possibilities rather than dictate what needs to be done.

You need to communicate your expertise in a confident but understated way, without seeming to be patronizing. Your experience, training, and knowledge will speak for themselves. Resist the temptation to detail your credentials, show off, or say you've done this before. While you might think such talk will burnish your credibility, it will actually diminish your legitimacy.

"The Right Place at the Right Time"

Sometimes credibility comes not from an academic degree that you have but because you are in the right place at the right time. By being in the right place at the right time, you find yourself with access to people, information, and knowledge that aren't available to others. Sometimes you can stumble into a situation that lends you credibility.

Arthur Fry, a young product development researcher at 3M (then called the Minnesota Mining and Manufacturing Company) stumbled into a situation where he earned instant credibility. Active in his church choir, Fry routinely bookmarked his hymnal but found that bookmarks were unsatisfactory, as they tended to slip out from between the pages. Fry knew of a weak adhesive that a colleague had developed a few years previously and that was sitting in 3M's vaults. He applied the adhesive to his bookmarks, and they kept his page without falling out or ruining the pages of the book. With his insight, he was able to marshal the company's resources and rally a coalition of chemists and engineers to develop the Post-it note.

If you happen to be in the right place at the right time, you must be able to move quickly to translate your spontaneous insight into a concrete agenda. Your challenge is to convince others you know what you're talking about and present the opportunity in a way that doesn't threaten the position of others.

"It Comes with the Turf"

Positional authority means that you have the organizational influence to put your agenda in place. While others might have insight and sway, you can move an agenda simply because of your role in the organization. If you've climbed the organizational ladder, the assumption is that you have the relevant expertise and clout to make things happen.

Positional authority is a double-edged sword. You don't want to point to your uniform or your role in the organizational hierarchy too often. You want this type of credibility to be supplementary and understated. You want people to know that you have the capacity to move things without flaunting your status. Authority of this type must be subtle. Use it too often and your credibility will be reduced to autocracy. You don't want your coalition building to boil down to "Join my effort—or else!" Rather, you want to suggest the opposite: "If you join the effort, if you join the campaign, I will use my organizational clout to get behind you, our group, and our ideas." You want to convey a sense that if others join you, you will use your organizational strength to make sure that everyone gains. You want to make it clear that if they are on your side, you are on their side too.

All is not lost if you don't have positional authority. You can leverage other types of credibility, such as expertise, to gain the support of someone who has legitimate positional authority to bolster your position. Sell your idea to others with positional authority, such as Top Dogs, Gatekeepers, or Gurus, and show them that combining your expertise and coalition with their positional authority will make things happen. Make sure they know that they will share the credit. With a boost of positional authority, you can go back to your potentials and give them confidence that you have internal support for your idea.

"I Can Be Trusted"

To sell an idea and mobilize a coalition, personal integrity is fundamental. Potential coalition partners will endorse your agenda only if they believe your proposal is not governed by your own self-interest but by your interest in the organization as a whole. Even if they have questions about the details, they will nonetheless feel secure that your efforts are ultimately worthy of collaboration and joint action. Integrity can help you support a sustained campaign that can overcome organizational hurdles.

Your personal integrity will be judged by the history of your behavior in the organization. Candidly consider this history when you set out to form a coalition. Perhaps you were once involved, even peripherally, in an episode of office politics that left some colleagues upset and bitter. Perhaps you once, in an unguarded moment, unkindly disparaged a colleague's work. If your integrity can be questioned at all, try to bring in others with unblemished histories to join you. Such partners can become important spokespersons for your coalition and your agenda.

Think of integrity as your agenda's insurance policy. Your reputation of integrity serves as reassurance for tepid coalition partners and can keep skeptics quiet even as uncertainty and resistance threaten to sink your agenda. As other sources of credibility ebb and flow in a volatile organizational world, your integrity is the buoy that keeps your coalition afloat.

▲ ▲ ▲

In the task of establishing your credibility and the credibility of your ideas, your words and actions will be equally important. Choose the former carefully. By thinking before you speak, you can show that your ideas are credible without appearing arrogant, obnoxious, and self-important.

Don't talk about your expertise. Demonstrate your expertise. Don't talk about your authority. Show through your words and actions that you can take the specific steps needed to get things done. Don't talk about your integrity. Your history in the organization and the real sincerity you express will lead to the results you want.

Your credibility can be tainted by others' negative perceptions of you and your intentions. If you are deemed too young, you may be credited with having technical knowledge but not enough authority or experience to move things forward. You need to demonstrate your capacity to learn quickly and an ability to be flexible.

If others think you have been around too long, you may be credited with knowing the intricacies of the organization but dismissed for not being current. You need to demonstrate your understanding of the technicalities and your ability to partner with individuals who have technical knowledge.

If you previously led a failed project or made a misstep in your career, you may have to work twice as hard to regain your credibility. Don't be put off by having to overcome more obstacles. Figure out where your weaknesses lie, and take steps to compensate for them. If your expertise, authority, or integrity is in question, think about what concrete actions you can take to show people that you have learned from your mistakes. At the same time, bring on board partners who are strong in the areas where you are weak—especially if resistance is high. Don't worry about sharing the limelight. If you need strong partners to overcome resistance, then bringing in those partners is a demonstration of your leadership, not an abrogation of it. You will be known as someone who can marshal the right people to carry an agenda through. That is part of what pragmatic leadership is about.

Gauge Your Support

Sure, you want them in your corner and on your side. You want them to be members of your coalition. The subtle question is: What kind of support do you want? It is easy to assume you want everyone behind you 100 percent. It is easy to scoff at anything but the most full-hearted support. Be careful! It might not be the gift you think it is.

Think about it. Maybe you don't want your supporters so enthusiastic that they become involved in every detail. If your supporters have insights or good ideas that can help move your plan forward, you want to hear them. But you don't want a bunch of people muscling in on your act, each sure that he or she knows a better way to do things.

Suppose you want to expand your organization's online presence in a big way. To move ahead in the online market entails an initial investment of $25 million. To make this idea a reality, you need the support of your board of trustees. But while you need the trustees on your side, you don't want them to get too involved. You don't want them to develop grand ideas that will derail your original purpose, and you don't want them to micromanage your effort. You want the trustees to give you active support—but not too active.

Support is likely to be active, passive, reluctant, or weak. In part, the type of support, and how strong it is, will depend on how others assess your credibility as a leader of the initiative. With measured use of pragmatic motivational skills you can enhance support where you need it the most.

In this context, you have two motivational approaches at your disposal. The first is to excite people about what you're doing—that is, get them to normatively accept the value of your initiative. The second is to convince them that it is in their benefit or the benefit of those they work with to actively join your effort. How you use these two motivational approaches will help determine the type and degree of support you'll receive.

Agenda movers understand that the danger of overmotivation is no less than the danger of undermotivation. If you aim too low, and undermotivate, you'll get an alienated, indifferent crowd. If you are unrelenting in your efforts to fire people up, you are likely to over

EXPECTED BENEFIT TO OTHERS	YOUR CREDIBILITY WITH OTHERS	
	Great	Small
Great	active support	passive support
Small	reluctant support	weak support

motivate and end up with a heavily involved troupe of micromanagers or a worshipful cult. It is between these poles that you as an agenda mover must search for support.

Active Support

People who actively support your initiative will do so because they trust you and believe in your ideas. They accept your ability, position, integrity, and unique perception of a problem. They also most likely believe that they (or their group, constituency, demographic, and so on) will benefit from your plan, either directly or indirectly.

To get active support, you have to remember that you're not recruiting cheerleaders but asking others to take an active role, even a small one, in a campaign. The active supporters of a politician don't just argue his or her merits around the dinner table. They do something to help that person win the election, whether making campaign donations, displaying a poster, volunteering for door-to-door canvassing, or writing a letter to the newspaper.

Active support is important in situations that require highly committed and motivated people. For example, pushing an agenda on a highly contentious political issue requires people who will volunteer their time and energy and be willing to work long hours.

There are two main risks inherent in securing active support. The first is that high-profile supporters might try to micromanage your campaign. The second is that supporters may come to expect more than you can possibly deliver or will tie you down to an inflexible agenda. If you oversell yourself and your idea, supporters may not be willing to compromise if circumstances change, and you must adapt your goals or your tactics to new conditions.

This is what happened to President Obama. During the 2008 election campaign, Obama's support among Democrats was very high. Through his speeches and record, he had established his credibility as someone with high intelligence, great compassion, moral fiber, and lofty goals. As a result, his Democratic constituency had enormous expectations from him as president. However, President Obama ran into the limits of the office and the realities of national politics and world affairs. By the 2012 campaign, Democrats' attitudes toward Obama had soured. Where once he had been regarded as nearly godlike, he was now understood to be a mere mortal, with human frailties.

The pragmatic leader is careful not to oversell. Establish your credibility and the credibility of your ideas, but don't promise the end of the rainbow. Agenda movers seek active support but keep it in perspective. They realize that ardent commitment by others may not always be a plus.

Passive Support

Passive supporters are drawn toward your agenda or plan because they can identify its benefits, but they have reservations about your credibility. They think your idea might work, but they question your capacity to go the distance. If you deliver what you say you can, they want to make sure they are able to reap some of the rewards.

Suppose you have a fantastic idea that you believe will improve workflow processes throughout your organization. Everybody you consult with thinks your idea will benefit their department. However, you're a relatively new hire, so nobody wants to stick their neck out in case you prove to be completely inept. That's fine. Passive support in this case may be just what you need. It means that colleagues won't get in your way and hamper your efforts. As long as you have active support from a few key stakeholders who can persuade the organization's decision makers that your plan is worth trying, you're in a good position. As your agenda moves ahead and shows some success, your passive supporters may move into the active column.

Think of passive supporters as free riders. They aren't in the business of making friends and backing grand visions. They provide neither assistance nor opposition, but they will stick around as long as they can expect to benefit from your plan. As an agenda mover, you will need to reiterate the expected benefits of your plan and show how each step is bringing those benefits closer.

Coalitions with a large roster of passive supporters are delicate. If perceived benefits dry up, passive supporters won't think twice about leaving a coalition.

Reluctant Support

Reluctant supporters say they are more than happy to help out or eager to lend a hand—but they wind up not lifting a finger. They like you. They believe in your credibility. They may even be your good friends. For whatever reason, they don't want to go on the record saying "no." In all honesty, they'd prefer to stay on the sidelines, because they don't expect to benefit much from your plan.

High credibility and low expected benefits is the recipe for reluctant support. Agenda movers understand that initially it may be hard to persuade others that they will gain concrete benefits from a given agenda—but they can show their credibility, and this may be enough to get people at least nominally supportive. The danger of initiating too many projects where the expected benefits are low and you have to rely on your credibility is that you risk repeated failure. No one bats a thousand, but if you consistently are unable to execute, your credibility is going to take a beating, and you are going to have to look for different avenues of support.

If you have a lot of power in the organization, reluctant support may come in handy if you want to bolster the size of your coalition—and if you don't need the reluctant supporters to do any work on your behalf. If all you need is an ability to show that you have others behind your initiative, reluctant support may be enough to get your idea off the ground. Remember that in the short term, a coalition of reluctant supporters may look solid, but in the long term, it may contain more cracks than an old painting.

If you know that the expected benefits for others are low, look for ways to increase the benefit factor. Offering enough attractive benefits could make reluctant supporters reassess their position in your favor.

Weak Support
When people believe your idea has little credibility and expect few benefits if you achieve your goals, they are likely to offer weak support. They want absolutely no responsibility for your campaign. They don't want to risk joining you, because, frankly, they think you

won't succeed. Therefore, they won't give you any public support, and they won't help in developing or spreading your ideas. If weak supporters mention your cause to others at all, they will do so out of a sense of fair play rather than a belief in the cause.

Weak supporters don't have much faith in your ability to get the job done. If they claim to support you—it may just come down to office politics. People may regard it as advantageous to be seen as someone who supports others rather than someone who is hard to please.

Agenda movers understand that they have to take it easy with weak supporters. Weak supporters cannot be overwhelmed and have to be brought along gradually. Remember that you may never move weak supporters to a more positive position, but you want to keep their support stable so they don't make the switch to resistors.

You are going to have weak support, and your challenge will be to keep it contained. Identify weak supporters as early as you can, and work to establish your credibility with them and to show them the expected benefits of joining your coalition.

▲ ▲ ▲

Support isn't a monolithic idea. Sometimes leaders go after 100 percent support from everyone and end up being overwhelmed by over-involved active supporters and discouraged by weak supporters. Or leaders can misread weak support for reluctant support, reluctant support for passive support, and passive support for active support. Agenda movers understand the subtle differences among the four types of support. They are aware of the importance of not overmotivating. They understand that the best way to move an agenda forward is to have a few active supporters, a strong core of passive supporters, a smattering of reluctant supporters, and a handful of weak supporters. Agenda movers understand the tactical importance of having a mixture of support. They know they don't need everyone on their side

▲ ▲ ▲

Mobilizing support is a key activity of agenda movers. As you learned in this part of the book, mobilizing support requires a degree of political competence. You have to be cognizant of how you focus the message, careful about timing your message, smart about the language you'll use, and perceptive about the audience you'll target. No matter how powerful you are, or how great your idea, you have to press into service each of these arguments to justify your initiative. Agenda movers understand that great ideas that are not grounded in justification may lead to resistance. Similarly, agenda movers don't assume their credibility or the credibility of their ideas. They prove it. Finally, while they need to mobilize support, agenda movers have to be careful to gauge the support they need. Support comes in various packages, and a politically competent agenda mover is able to discern one type of support from another.

Having achieved initial mobilization and gained their initial support, the agenda mover must negotiate the buy-in.

4

NEGOTIATE SUPPORT

Get the Buy-In

NEGOTIATE

What is initial support? Simply put, initial support is not a "no." If they haven't slammed the door in your face, you have some small reed of support you can grasp onto. However, if they haven't said "no," they haven't said "yes" either, and you can't count on them to shout out their support in a public arena. What you need to do is nudge them from initial support to true buy-in, and have them be a willing participant of your coalition.

Getting the buy-in is a process of negotiation and persuasion. You must tap the motivation of allies, potential allies, and resistors by discerning their potential motivation for joining you in your effort. You have to be careful not to confuse initial support with explicit support. Buy-in is explicit support. It is not subtle. It is easy for someone to give initial support because nothing has been exchanged, promised, or declared. Buy-in is quite different. Without buy-in, you have only vague statements. Without honest-to-goodness buy-in, you do not have a show of commitment or the seeds of a proactive coalition.

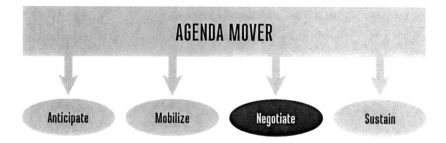

Getting the buy-in is about shifting your focus from sharing your passion for your idea to really thinking about where the other party is coming from. This does not mean that you put a damper on your enthusiasm, but what it does mean is that you have to move your attention to the other party or parties whom you need on board for your idea to really work. Getting the buy-in requires having an understanding of the intentions of others and a mastery of the negotiation process. Now is the time you want them to get behind your agenda. You want them to outwardly support your plan. For your potential supporters to take that last step, they have to come to understand that your proposed agenda is the correct course of action. They have to believe that there is a clear benefit not only for them personally but also for their unit or organization and the people they represent.

To gain their support, you have to reduce their anxiety, let them know what the benefits are for joining your coalition, set the tone, not shy away from making power arguments, manage the stage, and get the right mind-set.

Reduce Their Anxiety

There may be an abundance of reasons why they may not want to join your effort: a desire for economic security, the fear of failure, the inertia of habit, the lack of incentives, or the sense that doing nothing is the most comfortable thing to do. In asking people to join your coalition, you are asking them to change and to risk. You have to recognize that you are asking them to enter a place where they may feel unsafe or uncomfortable.

Moving an agenda, especially within the context of an organization, will inevitably create anxiety on the part of those whose support you need because there is a good chance that your agenda will impact them directly or indirectly. It is essential for the agenda mover to understand the nature of the anxiety underlying resistance. In virtually every organization, beneath the facade of cooperation, there is a cauldron of competing agendas and differing intentions. Whether at IBM or in Congress, the agenda mover must tease out the underlying fears that they are likely to bring about when they propose some sort of change or new innovation. As an agenda mover, you can better understand the underlying fears of others by thinking about how they will react to your agenda.

Clearly, how resistance manifests itself will depend on the nature of your idea. If your idea is revolutionary, thus requiring major changes, others may react with anxiety or hesitation. If your idea is a spinoff or refinement of an old idea, you might have better luck getting people on board. If you have a revolutionary agenda, it is unlikely that you will be able to overcome the resistance of traditionalists, unless you are able to change their mind-set and get them to see your agenda from a completely different perspective.

If you would like support from an adjuster (that is, someone who is committed to change, but all in good time) for your revolutionary idea, however, there are some steps that you can take. You might suggest that the changes be implemented incrementally or propose that the idea be developed or examined offline and brought online at some mutually agreed on date. If you want them to join your effort, you have to think deeply about their fears.

Recently, a CEO of a major corporation requested that a HRIS system be used to collect data across all corporate departments and all divisions. Putting his vice president of administration in charge, and with the collaboration of a major consulting firm, the goal was to create an integrated and highly automated HRIS system. The idea was not uniformly embraced, and some colleagues, like the head of marketing, were opposed from the very beginning.

The lead of the product services division gave the idea a tepid reception. It wasn't that he objected; he had already agreed to support the initiative when it was first introduced. However, the time had come to move beyond giving initial support, and he felt pressure to buy in and give public support. He had to go a step beyond tokenism. Realizing that the HRIS system was now close to reality, he hesitated. His was a large division that showed some profitability, but in private moments, he admitted his bottom line could be better. The last thing he needed was too much snooping around from the outside world.

The VP of administration, as head of the project, did not understand the fears of the lead of product services. The VP quickly coded the lead of product services as a two-faced obstructionist who reneged on his promises. The VP of administration didn't take the time to focus on the fears that others might have in accepting the new idea but instead kept pushing on the quality of the idea. The VP unwittingly pushed this adjuster lead of product services to join forces with traditionalist-minded marketing head who did not even want to hear about the HRIS system. Not surprisingly, the implementation of the HRIS system stalled.

Had the revolutionary VP been dealing with a developer, it would have been easier to find common ground. The developer would be both committed to change and interested in the agenda. What differentiates the developer from the adjuster is that the developer is more likely to endorse large organized change, while the adjuster prefers slow, incremental change. The VP of administration was in a bind. The traditionalists would not support him, and the adjusters and developers were looking for radically different things. How could he get them to join his coalition? This could happen only by understanding that resistance cannot be overcome by the endless repetition of the same justifications. Resistance can be mitigated, if not eliminated, by creating the right mind-set and by addressing their fears.

You may have a great idea, and they may actually want to join you. They may be enthusiastic. However, if you want their buy-in, you must give them a sense that they will both benefit and be safe. An agenda mover constantly focuses on the fears of those whose support he needs, most notably the fear of failure, the fear of the new, and the paranoia of turf encroachment.

The Fear of Failure

As an agenda mover, you must address the fear of failure. Agenda movers understand that a primary obstacle that they face is their own fear of failure. However, by the sheer fact that they are taking the lead, it is clear that they have developed the confidence to go beyond this concern. They view the success of moving their agenda as within the realm of reasonable probability. Their challenge in trying to get the buy-in from others is to get them to overcome their fear of failure and to see success as within the realm of reasonable possibility. By asking others to accept your agenda and coalesce around your effort, you are asking them to invest. You want them to invest time, effort, and perhaps resources into a project with an uncertain outcome (no matter how certain success seems to you). Given that most people are risk averse, the fear of failure is a source of anxiety and resistance.

The fear of failure seems so obvious as to be hardly worth discussion. Whether Lou Gerstner moving IBM from selling mainframes to solutions, or Steve Jobs trying to move the iPad, or the president of the United States pushing for health care reform, or a R&D chief executive for Cisco advancing mobile apps for live sports events, or any agenda mover, the possibility of failure looms large. In getting the buy-in from others, you need to help them face the fear of failure—you have to couch your intent in their reality. You have to view your agenda from their perspective. You need to illustrate how your agenda relates to their goals and aspirations. Beyond that, you have to be concrete. Ideas can be rejected because they sprawl or are too sweeping. Rein in the scope of your idea, and focus on exact costs and timelines. Don't allow the drama and power of your idea to make you promise more than you can deliver.

The Fear of the New

Another potent fear is the fear of the new. Fear of the new has a different dimension than fear of failure. Humans necessarily routinize behaviors, processes, and methodologies, and nowhere is this more evident than in organizations. Habit is a powerful motivator, and there is comfort in doing things the same way. With habit, people know what to expect, and anything "new" adds a layer of confusion. In organizations, patterned behavior becomes institutionalized and repeated, and when it is challenged, there is resistance: "That's not how we do things here." This fear is far more subtle than the fear of failure, and the agenda mover must deal with it directly.

In theory, many will not challenge a new direction. But when change actually starts—and routine, budgets, and work processes are discernibly different—people get conventional, fast. While people might say that they want new, innovative ideas, they may not be as receptive when dealing with the results.

A classic example of organizational change that deeply challenged the standing operational processes was Jeroen Van der Veer's major operation to simplify and integrate the IT processes throughout Shell, known as Downstream One. This unprecedented global upgrade took eighteen months to plan, affected over 37,000 users in thirty-six countries, and would be executed over a weekend.

To confront the fears of Shell employees, Van der Veer reached out to those who would be affected by the change to discuss risks and potential problems that the upgrade might bring about. Van der Veer was able to stress the important business impact of the project and that successful completion was a must. Van der Veer's ability to communicate—not only with Shell employees but also key external players—helped make the far-reaching IT agenda possible:

> SAP, IBM and other service providers had their top engineers on duty for the entire 48 hours. And a specialist IT team assembled at T-Systems offices in The Hague. These IT professionals did not have a concrete task at that time—they were on standby. Had an issue arisen, they would have been able to analyze and resolve it right away. [1]

Ensuring that key external players were ready to help with any disruption helped reassure Shell employees that they were well equipped to confront any sudden change that could possibly delay the upgrade: "It was a vital precaution, since failure to complete the migration would have disrupted Shell's business in key areas and meant the entire upgrade process would have had to be started all over."[2] By involving the external partners in the discussion, he was able to reduce Shell employees' fear of the new and get their buy-in. The upgrade was a success, in part due to Van de Veer's ability to allay the fear of the new.

The Shell example, while dramatic, illustrates some fundamental tactics that agenda movers must consider using when helping others overcome the fear of the new. You must be ready to reassure others, and expect that you'll have to do a certain amount of hand-holding. The anxiety stems from the fact that employees are collectively used to doing things the old way. If the rules or processes are changed midstream, people won't know exactly what to do or how to react in the new environment. People may be afraid of slipping up or not having the ability to make appropriate adjustments. In short, people don't want to look bad in front of their coworkers.

What Van der Veer understood is that there had to be strong or-ganizational support during this period of adjustment. When you are trying to get individuals to support your agenda, you need to delineate the very specific steps and resources you will make avail-able to support them during the transition. Hollow reassurances of "it's going to be okay" will not get them to support your agenda. You have to let them know on a concrete level that you will be there for them. Agenda movers need to make the unfamiliar feel somewhat comfortable if they want their new idea to become a reality.

The Paranoia of Turf Encroachment

Even if there is no hesitation due to the fear of failure or fear of the new, the agenda mover can stumble onto the paranoia of turf en-croachment. This is when individuals or groups are afraid they will lose their identity, power, and ability to control their own destiny. In the context of complex organizations where turf is both an obstacle and a reality, in order to get the buy-in an agenda mover will have to deal with the paranoia of turf encroachment. In doing so, however, an agenda mover must keep in mind the truism that "Just because you're paranoid doesn't mean you're wrong." In complex organiza-tions, it is very easy to lose control, identity, and power. As such, concern for keeping one's turf can be justified. Therefore, it is not unreasonable within today's world of streamlining that one be a bit paranoid before giving support to a new agenda.

The introduction of new ideas can create a shift in priorities and resources that will make some feel alienated, undervalued, or ner-vous. Broad change initiatives make it difficult for people to protect old turf and old ways of doing things. New ideas might imply an infringement on the status and power held before. An agenda mover must take these concerns seriously and think of ways to preserve the status and resources of key stakeholders while implementing the new agenda.

Upon returning to Apple in 1997, Steve Jobs saw and confronted turf paranoia firsthand. At this point in time, Apple was organized into sixteen different divisions with sixteen marketing budgets. Turf paranoia ran riot in this feudalistic set-up—and the challenge of making some kind peace among the warring factions was daunting.

Jobs knew that each division was critical to Apple's success, and he knew that to effectively drive his innovation agenda forward he would have to build cross-organizational support throughout Apple.

He combined the marketing budgets of all divisions not simply as an easy way to cut costs but to create a central space where decisions could be made and discussed with the involvement of every stakeholder, or rather, turfholder.

Jobs destroyed the paranoia of turf encroachment by creating an environment with no turf. This is not a widely applicable example, in that you aren't always able to clear the field and start fresh.

A better example of the paranoia of turf encroachment emerges in the situation of a merger or acquisition. Mergers can happen within organizations, but they often go by other names, such as "restructuring" or "centralizing" or "moving to the shared-services model." Mergers are complicated propositions to begin with, and may involve centralization, streamlining, integration, elimination of functions, and shifting identities. When merging two entities with the same goals—but perhaps with different cultures, processes, and structures, the challenge is greater, and there is understandably more turf paranoia.

A case in point is the merger of two medical providers. One is a university hospital, with academic faculty and a teaching institution, and the other is a larger provider of health care services. At first blush, it seemed like a marriage of equals. Independently, each institution has its own goals—to serve the patient. The secondary goals were to educate the doctors and researchers of tomorrow, to conduct research, and to make money. Together, there was the possibility of achieving economies of scale, securing better vendor pricing, limiting competition, and offering an array of treatment options to a larger geographic area. In addition, with a united front, they would be in a better position to weather changes in the health care industry. At the outset, it seemed like a win-win.

But the reality of the integration was rife with turf paranoia. Academic medical faculty bristled at being treated like salaried physicians. Staff objected when they were stripped of their tuition benefits. Nonaffiliated community doctors and hospitals were distressed by the creation of the new health care leviathan and engaged in passive resistance and declined to refer patients to physicians practicing in the new health care system.

There were many mistakes with this merger, but the biggest one was the discounting of the importance of turf. Staff needs went unrecognized and unnoticed. The turf of academic faculty was intruded on when the leadership ignored their faculty identity as teachers and researchers. The unaffiliated doctors and hospitals saw the new health care system as intruding on their turf and potentially harmful to their patients.

The lesson here is simple. While it may be necessary to break down turf to move an agenda forward, it is also important to assure individuals that their support of your initiative will not necessarily come with the loss of power, prestige, or control—in short, turf. What you need to do is to find a way to recognize and value every party involved and avoid giving them the sense that something is being taken away from them.

Engaging in turf protection makes very good sense. Recently, as universities have tried to move ahead to develop online learning, core faculty have become paranoid about their turf. They view themselves as the sole guardians of academic excellence. Faculties at major academic institutions initially saw, and continued to see, online learning as an invasion on their turf. It was a direct challenge to their power, their control, and their ability to direct their destiny, as pertaining to their research agenda. University administrators were often driven by the profit motive. Simply put, online learning is a financially beneficial endeavor. Faculty, in contrast, see it as a potential diminution of academic excellence, leading to the demise of the role of academic faculty, who over time, could be replaced by a platoon of adjuncts and learning designers. In this context, to many, the paranoia of turf encroachment seems justified.

At top-tier universities, however, faculty involvement is critical to the legitimization of online education as a tool for learning. Therefore, to get the buy-in for faculty to join the coalition for online learning, administrators and proponents of online education came up with several ideas that ensured not only faculty involvement but also mechanisms for faculty to have their turf. In some places, the compromise was to permit online education only for professional degrees. In others, it was used for certification programs. And in other places, it was decided that departments could choose whether or not to enter the online arena. In the instances where the most satisfactory solutions were reached, the paranoia associated with turf encroachment was dealt with by establishing trust one step at a time. That is what agenda movers need to do. They must move one step at a time to show the key stakeholders how they will keep their interests in mind. Assuring others that you have their interests in mind will help you to get the buy-in.

One or all of the three fears are likely to rise to the surface when you move from getting initial support to concretely negotiating the buy-in. The buy-in implies a stronger commitment than simple initial support and therefore is likely to stimulate a higher level of concern on the part of those you are trying to mobilize on behalf of your agenda. In this context, the agenda mover has to understand the underlying psychology of hesitation. Before you negotiate, before you try to move toward the explicit buy-in, you must be aware of the hesitation and the fears of others. Your task is to reduce their anxiety to give them a sense of safety and remind them of the potential payoff.

To achieve this, you must first couch your agenda in their reality. You always have to be thinking of your audience and their world. You need to illustrate your ideas by explaining how your ideas relate to their lives. You must next address their sense of risk. Often, leaders don't dwell on the inherent risks of their ideas when presenting them to the team. Take the time to identify areas of risk and ways risk can be mitigated. Be as specific and transparent as you can in sharing the details of your plan with others. And finally, you must accentuate prestige. Knowing that individuals will often resist change because they fear loss of status and turf, accentuate the social prestige and recognition that they will likely receive by joining your effort.

Dealing with their fears and reinforcing the potential payoff are ways of carefully moving them from initial support to concrete buy-in.

What's in It for Them?

When pitching your idea, you have to be prepared to answer the question, "What do I gain from joining your effort?" By showing that they have the smallest degree of self-interest doesn't mean that they have Machiavellian tendencies or that they are necessarily corrupt. It shows that they are rational human beings.

People generally do not go out of their way out of the goodness of their heart. In any organization there is a quota of do-gooders who are willing to do anything for the team, but for most people, there needs to be some external motivating factor to help them move out of their comfort zone and beyond the status quo. Your task, as an agenda mover, is to think about what would motivate them to join your effort. You have to think of what the other party will gain from joining your effort—and maybe the pleasure of your company isn't enough. Maybe they need a little something else you hadn't considered.

Remember, you are asking for something very precious—their support, and support can be manifested by perfunctory cheering from the sidelines or by a serious time commitment. Someone is not going to join you for the long haul for the fun of it or, literally, for nothing. You must negotiate coalition support. You have to be specific about the practical benefits the other party will gain from joining your effort.

Subjective expected utility is a term from economics that describes how people arrive at a decision that will give them the best chance of getting what they want. Whether people join your coalition will depend on the answer to "What's in it for me?" If the benefits of joining your coalition outweigh what they will gain by sitting on the sidelines, there is a stronger likelihood that they will join your coalition. If they feel that they will not gain or otherwise lose by supporting your effort, you can be sure that they won't be signing up anytime soon.

As an agenda mover, the topic of subjective expected utility might not be an academic notion you're aware of, but think about what you are trying to do. You are trying to get people to realize that it is beneficial for them to support the agenda you're trying to move. Note the notion of "subjective." The evaluation of whether to support you and join your effort, even after an initial positive reaction, will be based on the answer to the question, "What's in it for me?"—emotional, economic, political, and social.

One of the tools you have in negotiating coalition support is the payoff. You have to be concrete about the explicit benefit they will gain if they join your effort. To some ears, "payoff" sounds to be a bit calculated. And it is, but it doesn't mean that you are an evil genius. The other party is going to be strategic in deciding whether to join or support your effort, and they are going to engage in some calculations of their own. They are going to ask what's in it for them, their unit, and their team. You better be able to answer those questions.

In getting the buy-in, there are three essential components that agenda movers need to think about when considering how they will explain the payoff to possible supporters. It's easy to say that there will be some unspecified positive payoff at a later date, but you need to put in more of an effort. What do potential supporters empirically seek? Benefits, social credit, and avoidance of blame.

There are two types of benefits: tangible and intangible. Tangible benefits are often thought to have a monetary component—that is, more funds for a pet project of the other party or a raise for a key staffperson. But it could be something like a more desirable office or a better parking spot. Depending on your role in the organization, it may be difficult for you to find and distribute tangible benefits. Keep in mind that organizations are awash in intangible benefits, such as the opportunities for giving favors or political support. It takes a little creativity to come up with desirable intangible benefits, but in some cases, their worth is more than gold. In either case, tangible and intangible benefits can be exchanged explicitly.

Social credit is appropriate recognition. If the project succeeds, and if the innovation is put in place, then individuals want to make sure that their support for you is recognized and publicly celebrated, both socially and politically. Most important, they want credit for supporting an initiative at a time when it might have been difficult to back. They want some credit for their courage in giving their buy-in.

Sergio Marchionne became CEO of Chrysler in 2009 as part of the joint Fiat-U.S. government effort to turn around the struggling American auto giant. He realized that he had to change Chrysler's stagnant culture and entrenched bureaucracy to improve Chrysler's innovation potential.

To get his direct reports on board, Marchionne presented them with a smorgasbord of intangible benefits. If they followed his lead they would gain more power, autonomy, and political support. The executive team now had the authority to quickly approve innovative ideas as they saw fit. Within days of his appointment, Chrysler's momentum-killing bureaucracy was effectively replaced by a flat organizational structure that allowed the rapid upward movement of innovation. Profits rebounded as innovation flourished. As a result, the new Dodge Dart, that had not only great mileage but also a good price, came to market in fewer than thirty-six months, which is lightning speed in Detroit.[3]

By skillfully offering his executive team what he could—more power, autonomy, and political support—Marchionne was able to engineer Chrysler's turnaround success.

Last, if the effort fails, potential supporters want to make sure that they are not blamed or, at the very least, that they have coverage and that the blame is shared by all participants. There is truth to the old adage that success has many fathers and failure is an orphan. Your potential supporters may say things such as: "I want to support you, but if this does not succeed, I will pay the price" or "I want to support you, but I need a back door." As a leader you must be concerned with the coverage that you give others. Sometimes you need to give them political coverage and a back door they can duck out of if things go bad. You must make it clear to your possible supporters that as an agenda mover you are willing to share credit, but at the same time, you are willing to take responsibility for whatever happens on your watch. You may also need to build in an escape clause for them—a built-in reason as to why they supported your agenda when it was not clear that all their constituents would have done the same.

Lyndon Johnson understood the importance of providing political coverage for members of his coalition. Consider Johnson's successful efforts to pass the 1957 Civil Rights Act. He knew that he could not rely solely on the support of his Northern liberal allies to successfully back his agenda. There were simply not enough of them in the Senate. He had to persuade conservative Southern Democrats to join his coalition—and to get them on his side he had to provide coverage.

While many knew that a civil rights act would eventually be passed, few Southern Democrats were willing to take the initial step to support it. To make the proposition more attractive to the Southern Democrats, Johnson added an amendment that gave "a person charged with contempt for disobeying a judge's order—say, a white official trying to prevent blacks from voting—the right to a trial by jury (which in the South meant an all-white jury)."[4]

Although the addition weakened the bill, it provided adequate coverage for conservative Southern Democrats to support it. They could tell their constituents that the act did little to overturn the old Southern racial order. Johnson understood that passing this bill through the Senate mattered more than its relative strength and that the legislation would serve as a backbone for future civil rights laws.

In getting the buy-in, you have to convince your supporters that they will benefit, be celebrated, and not be blamed. Nowhere is this more important than in a large organization where a coalition attempts to move a new initiative or put in place a new innovation. This is especially true when resources are limited and failure is a possibility. The greater the possibility of failure and the scarcer the resources, the more the agenda mover has to be very focused on getting the buy-in.

Don't Be Afraid of Power Arguments

In trying to get the buy-in, you may have dealt with their anxiety and various fears and made it clear what's in it for them. What is now called for is a bit of a little power-political minuet, a dance that is often executed but rarely celebrated or even acknowledged because it flies under the radar and smacks of manipulation and Machiavellian machinations. That said, this dance is essential to getting the buy-in. This dance has two components, and both are very subjective. First is the dependence component. The other party clearly understands that you need them in your corner. That's a given, but now you have to present the situation in such a way that you convey some independence from them. You have to give them the sense that as badly as you want them in your corner, there are indeed other fish in the sea.

You have to give them a sense that you have other alternatives to gaining their support. The tactic is to give them a sense that you need them, but you are not desperate. You want to engage in the subtle dialogue of impression management. You want to subtly convey some independence, while not overplaying it. You want to give them a sense of the options, while at the same time having them understand that you value their support. Just a footnote here: Begging is not a sanctioned agenda mover tactic.

There are essentially four types of arguments that convey the message of semi- independence.

Priority Argument
Priority arguments are the agenda mover's effort to be a bit subtle about his or her priorities. This is the classic case that the more

desperately you show you want something, the more demanding the other party can be. For this reason, you may want to consider backing off a bit. This is not to say that you dismiss it, but instead you simply shift away. In the midst of attempting to get moderate Republicans to support their immigration agenda, Democrats could raise the possibility of shifting to their health care agenda. Showing the ability to reprioritize in the middle of your effort to get the buy-in could give the other party a sense that they should not overplay their hand. However, that being said, if you overplay yours then they might call you out for not being fully committed. Your challenge is to give the sense that you could reprioritize but would rather not, if possible.

Self-Enhancement Argument

This is in which you convey to the other party that your idea might be the best, if not the only, way to move an agenda forward. You must convince potential supporters that with your capacity and skill, the change innovation can be put in place. Remember, at this point you already have some initial support. The self-enhancement argument makes the case that there are very few alternatives to moving the agenda ahead.

Your job is easier if they already agree that your idea has merit. You just need to communicate that your agenda is the only sure way to move ahead and there really aren't other viable options out there. This argument works best with people who have expressed initial support. You just have to convince them that going with you is the best course of action.

Threat-to-Leave Argument

This signals that you have options, and you're not afraid to use them: "If you don't go with me then I'll get someone else." Essentially, this is an explicit warning that if they decide at this point to not give you their buy-in, then you'll simply get someone else's support. This is a simple notion, but it's important. What you're conveying is that while you would like their buy-in, there are other parties that have already given you initial support, and you're perfectly willing to go with them. Again, you have to be subtle. You have to convey to your possible partners that you would like to go with them if possible, but there are other partners to approach if they don't actually buy-in.

Consequence Argument

The consequence argument subtly conveys to the other party that if they don't go with your effort then there will be subtle yet important implications. You have to handle this argument with kid gloves. You may want to go so far as to say that if you are forced to go with another party then that will jeopardize your long-term relationship. You may want to give a sense that if they do not go with you now, then it will be difficult for you to support any of their future efforts. However, here again, it is essential to be subtle, yet not coy. You want to be reflective, while not threatening. The moment that you appear to have made an explicit threat is the same as making an explicit threat, with the consequence of permanently damaging the relationship.

Trying to get their buy-in has an explicit power-dependence component to it. Essentially, you are trying to present a subjective reality in such a way that your potential supporters begin to realize that you are not desperate and that they may not have as many viable alternatives as they had initially thought. However, there are two critical cautionary notes.

First, some failed agenda movers sometimes overplay their hand. They bluff, and they are called on it. When you tell someone that you can do without their support, there is the possibility that they may drop their backing altogether. Again, you want to make them feel that they are essential, but at the same time convey the sense you are not desperate.

Second, never let your independence arguments read as a threat. Negotiating the buy-in occurs within the nuance of language. Yes, you want to convince them that you are not desperate, and that your agenda is their best alternative. That said, you never want to threaten them. The moment you do, you create a conflict that may spiral out of control. They'll either play tit-for-tat or the more dangerous "I'll-show-you" game. Once that happens, there is no hope that you will be able to transfer their initial support to real buy-in. They will not join your coalition. There is no recovery from threat. In the dooms-day scenario, they will become your worst enemy and actively work against your agenda.

Manage the Stage

Politically competent agenda movers are sensitive to tone and place. That is, they appreciate the dramaturgical context of where they choose to negotiate. The stage can send a very clear message. Meeting casually on a park bench connotes both informality and privacy. Meeting one-on-one in a noisy restaurant conveys less paranoid privacy. And the proverbial smoke-filled room sends another message. Obviously the tone and place are enmeshed, but all three have a role in creating the context of the buy-in process. Agenda movers are deeply aware of the nuanced messages they are sending. They are, in short, brilliant stage managers.

In trying to get others to coalesce around your agenda, you must also consider your tone and demeanor when meeting with the other party. Tone can complement the environment and control the openness of dialogue. What nuances do you want to give the interaction?

How informal or formal do you want to be? An informal interaction lets you be more personable, casual, and intimate. A formal interaction allows you to keep some distance between yourself and the other party and to hide behind your role.

Depending on your goal, an informal environment could be ideal—dropping into someone's office or heading out for a drink. An informal setting gives you the ability to slip your negotiation into the context of a friendly encounter. Of course, the fact that you haven't dropped any hints that you're about to negotiate also means that if you end up discussing more granular issues, the other party might not be ready, and therefore might not be prepared to give you what you'd like.

In an informal setting, you'll also be able to gauge the response of the other party without putting too much on the line. If your colleague is totally opposed to your idea right out of the gate, you'll have time to go back and rethink your approach. The other party might also sense that you are on a fact-finding mission. Another benefit of the casual, informal negotiation is that you can offer your colleague the opportunity to work on the problem with you. Together, you say, you will find a solution to offer to the larger group. This way, you can give the other party the space they need to figure out what they want before going public. An informal setting and tone might be a good choice if you want to test the waters before you set a formal process in motion. It is a good environment to introduce new ideas with the intention of getting serious about them later on.

An informal negotiation is just that—informal. There will be no ironclad agreement. The best outcome is a general agreement that you will work out a solution to the problem or issue, and move ahead together. The worst outcome is that you go back to square one, do some more work on your approach, and figure out what compromises you'll need to make before negotiating for real.

You could decide that formal negotiations would be more appropriate in trying to move your agenda. The symbols and ceremony of a formal agenda negotiation practically scream, "Warning: negotiation in process." The level of mutually expected preparedness defines formal negotiations. Generally, the parties in a formal negotiation head into it with a readiness to spell out costs, a specific timetable, and deliverables. When it is time to move on an issue, a formal negotiation signals that the process is serious, and the expectation is that the end result will have implications for everyone involved. If you do reach an agreement, there will be no questions over who does what and when. A formal negotiation can result in a clear game plan for both parties.

Typically, the tone of the discussion and the environment in which the discussion takes place are aligned, especially when your intention is to send a clear and consistent message. Sometimes environment and tone are not aligned. These situations may catch you off guard. Imagine walking into a formal office environment to discuss specific issues, only to be greeted by an informally dressed executive who tells jokes, asks about the family, and invites you to play a game of chess. Where is the message: in the formality of the environment or in the casual tone? You've probably been in the opposite situation, too. You go to an afternoon meeting in a park expecting the discussion to be informal and laid back. Instead, you're grilled about your department's productivity.

Again, where is the message? Setting and tone don't always need to be aligned. Such mixed messages are a way of maintaining control over the situation by keeping the other party off guard. In either instance, it's probably not clear what message the other party is trying to send, which can easily put you off balance. It is essential to keep in mind that mixed-messaging could be the result of conscious impression management.

How do you decide which type of environment and tone you want for your negotiation? Remember, impression management is not about the importance of the issue. It's about the message you want to send to the other party. The reason to choose one message over another is because you believe that particular message will give you a tactical advantage.

While preparing for speech on his position on civil rights to Congress, Lyndon Johnson gathered his advisors around his dining room table. By opening the conversation in an informal setting he allowed for deliberation. One of his advisers remarked that "a President shouldn't spend his time and power on lost causes, no matter how worthy those causes might be and Johnson replied, 'Well, what the hell's the presidency for?'"[5] Using the tone and setting the stage, Johnson was able to convey the sheer importance of his civil rights agenda while extinguishing any doubt regarding his motives.

Johnson took careful consideration of place and tone. He used a small room adjacent to the Oval Office, dubbed the "Little Lounge," as a place to rest and recuperate after one of his heart attacks. It's been noted that "Johnson felt that the lounge provided an informal and intimate setting to conduct business,"[6] testament that he knew that the "Johnson treatment"[7] worked better on certain people in an intimate setting. Johnson managed both the environment and tone as tools in getting his agenda across.

One of the most brilliant examples of this is Jimmy Carter's effort to move his agenda by getting Anwar Sadat and Menachem Begin to negotiate. Carter, knowing full well the historical tension between both parties, thought that it would be best for them to meet in a casual, intimate environment that could be controlled, and Camp David filled the bill on all counts.[8] Carter was astutely aware of the importance of stage management. In trying to move an agenda, where you meet the other party matters.

A politically competent agenda mover has to be a stage manager. This is especially true when you are trying to get the other party to buy in to your agenda and explicitly join your effort. At this point, setting the stage and managing your tonality is essential. Some of the greatest political leaders and successful corporate executives are masters of this very fine art. They understand that sometimes a casual discussion next to the metaphorical water cooler is more effective than one in the formal setting of an appropriation hearing. They understand that before they move negotiations into a formal setting to achieve closure, they need a series of informal discussions to build the dialogue that will lead to a formal coalescing around an idea. Mastering impression management is a key trait of an agenda mover.

Get the Right Mind-set

In any setting when you are trying to move your agenda, move people to your side, and achieve concrete support, the mind-set you bring to the situation will often dictate the outcome. How you approach the situation and frame it in your mind is essential. Politically competent leaders are careful not only in how they view the situation but also in how they present it to others. Agenda movers sometimes think along a continuum of two mind-sets when trying to get the buy-in. At one end, there is the hold-them-captive mind-set and on the other end is a pull-them-in approach.

In the hold-them-captive mind-set, you are not at all concerned about what will happen to the relationship after your initiative is in place. You're not concerned with making a lasting impression or gaining favor. This is all fine and good if you only need the support of the other party for one particular issue. If this is a one-time deal, you do not have to handle supporters and potential supporters with kid gloves. If you will not need their support down the road, you essentially have nothing to lose by taking the hardline approach.

You will use your power and make sure that everyone understands that you are in control. You will let them know that you prefer to move your agenda with them, but if they are unwilling or unable to get onboard, you will go around them.

In the pull-them-in approach, you view the other party as sharing some common core values and a common orientation to your position, and, in turn, you feel that you can negotiate a common solution and move together incrementally in a long-term coalition. You bring a noncaptive mind-set that shows you want to pull them in and establish a win-win that, in the worst case, will minimize loss. A pull-them-in approach is associated with problem-solving and conflict resolution. In this situation, the agenda mover does not resort to threats but reduces risk by emphasizing a common solution.

The negotiations that took place among the CEOs of the big banks during the 2008 financial crisis used elements of both the hold-them-captive mind-set (with unsuccessful results) and the pull-them-in mind-set (with successful results).[9]

At the onset of the financial crisis, the federal government had helped to engineer the buyout of a collapsing Bear Stearns to JPMorgan. A second bank, however, Lehman Brothers, began to collapse as well. Unwilling to allow the federal government to intervene again, Hank Paulson, the United States Secretary of the Treasury, gathered the CEOs of the largest banking institutions for a weekend of negotiations. Paulson's agenda was to have the CEOs of each bank invest in the toxic assets that ultimately led to Lehman Brothers' collapse. Essentially, he wanted them to buy a portion of these assets to spread the risk in Bank of America's proposal for a Lehman buyout. The deal would become much more favorable with their collective investment. Bank of America would not have to bear the entire risk of a merger failure resulting from the entire value of the toxic assets that it would otherwise have to swallow.

Initially, Paulson quite literally had a hold-them-captive mind-set. At the very beginning, he told the CEOs that he would remember those who were not helpful. The implication was clear: the banks that refused to cooperate would be on their own in the future, even if they showed a need for external help if the crisis worsened. He knew that none of the CEOs wanted to initially cooperate with his plan. He deduced that their acceptance of his agenda would result in their collective loss. For this reason, Paulson took the initiative to act in a pragmatic and Machiavellian manner. As the secretary of the treasury, he knew that he influenced much of the financial actions of the federal government. He was calling the shots. Therefore, Paulson had the ability to not give them a choice. He chose to initially force the banks to adopt his agenda of collectively investing in Lehman's toxic assets. As events turned out, Paulson's hold-them-captive approach did not sweeten the pot and did not encourage the CEOs to get on board with his plan.

Nearing the final day of negotiations there was still no agreement as to how Paulson's agenda of dividing Lehman's toxic assets among the banks would be implemented. Time had flown by; its passage was marked by a constant stream of bickering. At this point, Jamie Dimon, CEO of JPMorgan, suggested that each bank invest in the toxic assets. Dimon stated that JPMorgan would place the initial toxic asset investment. He then looked around the room to see if anyone else would join him. Lloyd Blankfein, CEO of Goldman Sachs, immediately followed suit. Others soon fell into line.

While this was not Dimon's party, he took the lead with a pull-them-in mind-set. After spending most of the weekend deadlocked, Dimon correctly understood that the implementation of Paulson's agenda would require the self-imposed mutual cooperation of the bank CEOs. Hours of squabbling proved to Dimon that Paulson could not simply impose his agenda—even though he possessed substantial power. Dimon realized that that the CEO collective had to mutually agree for the plan to be successfully implemented. By advocating for mutual toxic asset investment among the banks and agreeing to be the first to pledge investment in the toxic funds, he brought in the pull-them-in mind-set, and others quickly followed suit.

Without a toxic asset investment strategy, Lehman would collapse, and the repercussions would reverberate on the economy for years to come. No one wanted to take that initial step of advocating and agreeing to Paulson's agenda. Dimon's support and investment initiative was exactly what the CEOs needed to get on board with the plan.

Paulson had trouble making his hold-them-captive negotiation mind-set work. But Dimon, even though he was a guest at the table, was able to use a pull-them-in mind-set. Remember, even though the other party may try a harsh tactic, you don't have to play the game the way the board is set. You can be imaginative and use the mind-set that works best for you and your situation.

Another example of both mind-sets can be found in the history of health care reform in the United States. Bill Clinton was not able to reform health care in 1993 because he attempted to use the hold-them-captive mind-set to single-handedly see it through. He did not attempt to deliberately gain and grow the support that he needed to create an effective health care coalition.

During his first term, Clinton overestimated his power and didn't hesitate to alienate his resistors. He sent the message not only to Congress but also to the American public that he could do it alone. His supporters in Congress introduced many health care proposals, but the Republicans killed every one.

Clinton learned some hard lessons from his inability to push through a health care reform package. He learned to not overestimate his power, and he learned that the hold-them-captive mindset doesn't always work. In his second term, he was a better agenda mover. He was able to build a bipartisan coalition of support for his agenda, from welfare reform to balancing the federal budget.

Just as Clinton learned from his first-term mistakes, so did Obama. From the beginning, Obama did not overestimate his power. He knew he couldn't do it alone, and knew the value of a coalition. He used health care as a campaign issue, perhaps with a bit of the hold-them-captive mind-set, but he simultaneously applied the pull-them-in mind-set to gain the support necessary to build the congressional coalition that he needed for the bill to pass.

Through the combination of direct action, compromise, and a hands-off approach, Obama mustered the support to create a health care reform coalition, and ultimately the Affordable Care Act passed.

As you move your agenda, you have to think about which mind-set is best for your situation. Using the hold-them-captive mind-set, you may get people to join your effort, but you risk losing the opportunity to build a long-term relationship that can serve you in the long run. The pull-them-in, cooperative mind-set allows you to build support not only for your current agenda but also any agenda you want to pursue in in the future.

Here lies the primary political dilemma: What mind-set do you choose, and when? Politically competent agenda movers use both.

▲　▲　▲

An agenda mover understands that there is a difference between getting initial support by informally getting people on their side and getting the actual buy-in. A buy-in implies an alliance and partnership. As an agenda mover, you therefore must negotiate the buy-in and directly deal with the anxiety and fears that others may have. Any change, any innovation, no matter how positive it seems to you will inevitably raise angst in others. You must concretely deal with this. Having reduced their fears and anxieties, you must focus on the fact that people are going to want to know what's in it for them. Show them the benefits. Don't be afraid to make the type of arguments that will enhance their sense that this is a good opportunity for them. While doing this, agenda movers try to control the context and nuances of the negotiations. Agenda movers understand that getting the buy-in is essential and well worth the mindful effort.

5

SUSTAIN YOUR CAMPAIGN

Get Things Done

SUSTAIN

You've heard about the entrepreneur who has everything in place—the right team, the right support—but somehow drops the ball. You've seen the politician who promises change during the campaign but fails to deliver once he or she is in office. It is one thing to get elected. It's another thing to deliver.

As an agenda mover, you've already mobilized people around your ideas and won them over, but now the challenge is to get things done. You have to convert the energy of mobilization to the energy of implementation. You have to deliver. You have to sustain the coalition. Agenda movers understand that sustaining momentum is the true test—that is, when their ideas are institutionalized and can make a real impact. The challenge is to sustain the coalition—to make sure that it doesn't fall apart, that people don't drift away, that commitment is maintained, and that you actually get something done.

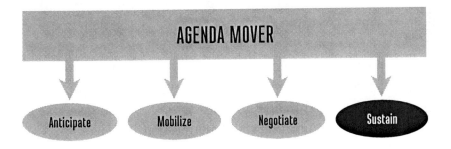

One common mistake that agenda movers make is to devote the bulk of their energy on developing the ideas and getting initial support, but their enthusiasm flags as they approach the finish line.

While political competence is still important at this stage, the agenda mover must hone his or her managerial competence to sustain forward movement and achieve impact. Agenda movers make sure that their coalition becomes a focused, agile, coordinated, forward-moving team.

No matter how politically competent you are or how well you mobilized others around your idea, you now need day-to-day managerial skills to make sure they go the distance. Managing to sustain your team's forward movement is just as important to leadership as anticipating and mobilizing. You may have sold your idea and created a coalition, but you can only sustain momentum and get results if your team can keep up its energy and focus in spite of challenges, obstacles, and setbacks. This means you have to create traction, pivot to make adjustments, manage with agility, bolster the coalition mind-set, and remain politically astute.

Create Traction

When enthusiasm is at its peak, it may seem as though the momentum will be self-sustaining. This is not the case. As an agenda mover, you must now create traction.

As you try to move your agenda down the road, you want your coalition members to feel some sense of accomplishment and to understand that supporting your effort was not a pipe dream. One of the challenges that entrepreneurial firms face is how to sustain momentum in a risky situation where gratification, if there is any, will be delayed. While the work is continuous, the light at the end of the tunnel somehow doesn't shine brightly. Similarly, in any social movement, traction is essential to give the participants the sense that the agenda is moving ahead.

Having traction will give your team the sense of the possible, reinforce the credibility and viability of your ideas, and sustain and energize your campaign. Small wonder that even in politics the public looks for small victories as an indication of long-term possibility. Having the sense that the light at the end of the tunnel is getting brighter will build confidence in your agenda and can lead people to be a bit less risk averse. Sure, they still support your effort, but they need some kind affirmation that they made the right decision to support you. There are two simple ways to achieve traction: marking short-term victories and validating your ideas.

Score Small Victories

In creating traction, nothing is more important than a sense of forward movement. Agenda movers appreciate that the best way of creating traction and building a sense of the possible is by accumulating small victories.

Overly ambitious leaders make the misstep of trying for too much, too soon. They come out of the gate running and expect to win the race hands down. Such leaders run the risk of burning out their initial supporters.

Large, complex agendas and visionary ambitions tend to be overwhelming. There is something to be said for the "one-step-at-a-time" mentality—with each step enhancing both traction and confidence.

In research and development, taking three steps back to move two inches forward is not uncommon. But indeed, those two inches are important, whether they are concrete or symbolic. In research, two inches may be a mile if the timing is correct. Your team may have tried every avenue and may be on the verge of frustration or even defeat when one nuanced victory turns the whole project around. Small victories, then, especially when they are well timed, can be essential to keeping your team together.

As an agenda mover, you might have to search for small victories. Once you find them, celebrate them. They may not be much, perhaps a spark or two, not a full-blown flame, but they will be enough to keep people going. For instance, if you're trying to build your online customer base, hitting the first 1,000 customers (or the first $10,000 in sales) might be worth a bottle of bubbly in the office. If you're introducing a new IT system, spread the word and thank your staff when the last department goes online or the last cohort of employees completes training. If you're developing a new product and it's not going well, gather your team for a congratulatory pep talk whenever there's a small advance.

Not only will small victories help you solidify your team by sharing a sense of common purpose and accomplishment, such celebrations can help make sure that others in the organization take note of your progress. Small yet visible victories will confirm the viability of your idea, validate the competence of your group, reinforce your capacity for execution, and justify the legitimacy of your agenda. Of course, the opposite might occur if you build up small advances as being much more important than they really are. But sharing a sense that something exciting is being kindled is a legitimate strategy for keeping other stakeholders on board, as well as strengthening morale among your team.

Agenda movers understand the essence of Hemingway's advice to writers: Get five hundred words a day on paper. Then each day will be a small victory of a sort. Each day will renew your strength, hope, and sense of progress. And as American politicians understand, you have to prove yourself in Iowa and New Hampshire so you have the momentum to win Florida, Ohio, and California.

Validate Your Ideas

Traction demands that your ideas be validated and legitimized by others beyond your core team. To sustain forward movement, your ideas need to expand beyond your initial group. It is essential to make sure your ideas do not become the sole province of your team.

For your team to have a sense of forward movement, they need confidence that key stakeholders outside the team accept the direction they're heading. You and your team need to keep others informed of your core efforts. You also need to be receptive to input from others outside the team.

In the push to move forward, you may be tempted to focus solely on what your team is doing and what it needs. It is difficult to overcome these tendencies. But networking and diffusing your ideas are essential for gaining the validation necessary for traction. Your team's morale will be higher if it has the sense that the rest of the organization is rooting for its success. More important, remember that any organizational team is part of a complicated influence network. To keep your project on track, you will need to make sure your initiative is grounded in the larger organizational context.

Diffusing your ideas beyond your base of support will take time, effort, and active networking. Connect with other people. Reach out to different groups and let them know what you're doing. Be proactive. If you hear that someone likes your idea, set up a meeting to fill them in. But remember that you won't be able to do all this work yourself. Supporters of your agenda have to be able to translate your message to have it legitimized outside of your coalition.

In this context, your primary concern in establishing validation of your ideas and traction is to increase the number of people in the influence network who are favorably disposed to your project. Networking with key actors will help you create and maintain traction in moving your agenda forward. Explicit support from the CEO (Top Dog), senior managers (Gatekeepers), staff members (Players), and outside experts (Gurus) can help ensure that your ideas are accepted across the organization. If you remain isolated with your team, others will regard you and your effort with indifference and apathy at best, suspicion and cynicism at worst.

Agenda movers constantly ask themselves: Who else do we need? Where else should we carry our message? By keeping these questions in mind, you can avoid inertia, isolation, and groupthink.

Today, universities face unprecedented challenges. At a major research university, a recent effort was undertaken to mobilize a team of academics, administrators, and a few trustees to move the university into an entrepreneurial venture with several high-tech companies. The leaders of the effort mobilized resources and negotiated key details, but they didn't bother to ensure that their ideas gained traction through the wider university community. They regarded proselytizing as beneath them and not essential to achieving the goals of the group. They believed they had a strong team and that this would give them all the traction they needed.

The failure of the core team to diffuse their message meant that outsiders viewed the team to be elitist and insular. Eight months into the process, the team faced serious resistance. Only then did the team begin to network, desperately seeking support from the broader university community. In the end, they managed to keep resistance from killing their project, but the team's inability to network early on slowed down progress on the project considerably.

New leaders often make the mistake of neglecting to have others outside their immediate circle validate their ideas. As they rise to the top, they feel that they have a mandate. Closely working with their own teams and staying committed to their agenda, they experience tunnel vision. Caught up in their new role and exhilarated by their desired direction, they forget to network with others. By the time they realize their agenda is stumbling it finally dawns on them that they need external validation of their ideas. The new leader could have shielded himself with an honest effort to gain traction through network validation.

Agenda movers know that ongoing networking is essential to sustaining a campaign. How can others support your plan if they don't know what you're doing?

Manage with Agility

As you try to move your agenda ahead so that your ideas become grounded and achieve success, it is important that you focus on your management style. As an agenda mover, you are responsible for managing forward movement. That means you have to be constantly aware, perpetually making adjustments, and always agile. Agenda movers know that they can't just walk away. They just can't inspire people and let the cards fall where they may; they have to deal with the grittiness of management, and that means being smart about how they present themselves and deal with others.

They understand that their primary drive is to sustain movement to get things done. They have people in their corner, and now they need to be engaged in the microdemands of managing for execution. Successful agenda movers are agile managers. They pivot to make adjustments, juggle their leadership style, control the dialogue, are smart about resources, and define parameters.

Pivot to Make Adjustments

Agenda movers need to learn the importance of pivoting to make adjustments. It is important not to overreact. Imagine you are in the early stages of putting your agenda in place, and a glitch arises in the beta testing. Is your first impulse to get the programmers on the phone and start yelling? Or do you understand that this is part of the process and know that by engaging in a problem-solving approach, things will settle down? Overreactive leaders frequently misread and misinterpret data and as a consequence can cause a lot of drama.

Leaders who overreach rather than having a measured, reflective action are under the delusion that any activity—even over-the-top frenzied behavior—is synonymous with action and moving ahead. They defend themselves by telling their detractors that they "did something."

Overreactive leaders love making bold, varied moves, but they often fail to realize that they drain momentum from the larger team. These leaders don't let the car build up speed but instead prefer to jerk the wheel with the hope of finding shortcuts. The risk, of course, is that they'll slow a team's progress or get lost.

Those who work with overreactive leaders sometimes suffer from whiplash. The constant change of direction can become exasperating. If they can't finish any projects they'll never receive full job satisfaction. An agenda mover needs to assure that their people aren't always wondering what's going to happen next week. They need to ensure some degree of stability. They can't continuously alter goals, priorities, and initiatives. Agenda movers are allowed to alter the course of the ship, but they can't create routine emergencies. It'll kill momentum and drive people to calmer shores.

When you have to make a change, make sure that you don't resort to finger pointing. You need to make tweaks, but you don't want to step on any toes. Make suggestions and pointers without making personal attacks. Your target is to give appropriate feedback without ruining the momentum. Remember you don't want to drive off a cliff—you want to get to the finish line.

Agenda movers have to make informed adjustments and translate them in a clear, constructive way. Pivoting is important, but you must never panic.

Juggle Your Leadership Style
In sustaining the momentum of your campaign, you have to be mindful of your leadership behavior. As an agenda mover, you un-

derstand that you cannot simply walk away from your campaign, but you have to stay involved. The question is, to what degree do you want to be involved? How are you going to lead your campaign to get things done?

Are you going to be directive, or are you going to be facilitative? While these are not mutually exclusive, you will have to consider which style to use when.

If you decide to be a directive leader that means that you want to move the agenda forward by holding the reins tightly. You believe that your capacity to get things done is to stay on top of the campaign. You believe that the agenda will be moved if you stick with the program, remain with the plan, and have some managerial control over the situation.

Embedded here is the notion is that if the campaign is going to sustain momentum and result in implementation, then it is your responsibility to coordinate, drive, and supervise the activity to make sure the goals are achieved. In this context, the emphasis is on accountability and predictability—tell them what to do, lay out expectations, and stay on top of the game. If you choose to lead your group in this way, you are likely to believe that you have the right ideas, the right people, and that things are relatively predictable. Keeping the focus on your target is the best path to success.

At the same time, things might not turn out the way you expected. You may have to make adjustments and rely on the individual creativity of your team members. You may not be able to cover all the bases. You may have to make decisions under the gun as you adapt to new situations. New challenges, new competitors, new markets mean that you need to make rapid and quick adjustments. Your planned path may become a zigzag of chaos. You are going to have to rely on individuals on your team to make decisions to get things done on their own and not just have them constantly check in with you at every turn. In this instance, directive leadership is unlikely to succeed. As an agenda mover you want people to feel assured in their ability to think on their feet and problem solve. You want to facilitate out-of-the-box thinking so inertia doesn't set in and work doesn't become a mindless routine.

Your best bet is to lead as a facilitative coach, to engage and enhance your team but not explicitly direct them. Facilitative leaders often abandon the traditional hierarchical organizational model and instead prefer a networked organizational structure. Team members solve problems rather than operate within strict job descriptions and set goals.

The facilitative leader depends on an informal exchange as opposed to top-down authority. They engage in the dialogue of coaching and are able to enhance the capacity of others by listening and engaging them. At their core, facilitative leaders do not shy away from the empowerment of their teams as the best way to get things done, especially in complex environments. They understand the paradox that to have control they must let go of certain things.

It is easy and somewhat foolish to say that directive leaders are micromanagers and facilitative leaders are passive and laissez-faire. This is not the case. Agenda movers are extremely mindful of leadership as a series of dramaturgical choices. They understand that how they both present themselves and take control are critical to getting things done. In certain situations, they may select to act one way; while in others, they may choose to act differently. Agenda movers understand that leadership is not just who they are but how they behave. This is a choice they can make at any point in time.

Juggling directive and facilitative leadership is what agile leadership is about. Even before agile leadership was in vogue as a term, pragmatic agenda movers understood that they had to move between taking control and letting go. They understood that agendas are able to achieve results when leaders know how to juggle between being directive and facilitative.

Control the Dialogue

As you move your agenda along, you will have to meet and discuss—not only with your team, but with others. Discussion and dialogue is part of moving ahead. You may not be able to move ahead exactly as you want to, and you ask your chief-of staff to call a meeting.

The chief-of-staff is willing to have the meeting, but wants to specify parameters, set a time limit, and start with the agenda in place. The others invited to the meeting understand the broad agenda, but they have their own agendas and issues. Unfortunately, the meeting chair is too facilitative. After forty minutes, it becomes clear that the agenda has long since crashed and burned. Everyone wants to put their issues on the table, and the discussion degenerates into several smaller, simultaneous conversations. The meeting chair tries to wrest back control but doesn't want to be abrupt; others try to help him focus the discussion, to no avail. After two hours, the meeting ends with an agreement to meet again.

In trying to get results, dialogue is essential. Processing ideas, brainstorming, and engaging in continuous open discussion are critical. Virtual and real meetings are the modus operandi of organizational life. Certainly the internet, webinars, and video conferencing haven't diminished the need for meetings; they've increased it.

One organizational leader reminisced, "In the old days we had meetings on Friday afternoons. It was the best logistical time for everyone. It seems now that we meet at the drop of a hat. It seems now everyone is asking 'Why didn't I call for a meeting? Why don't we dialogue?' In the old days at least I had a distancing excuse. Nowadays, a no-meeting day is a rarity."

Whether the emphasis on discussion and meetings in today's organizations is good or bad, as a pragmatic leader you need to know how to facilitate focused discussions. Well-planned, focused meetings can ensure that critical input is gathered and that adjustments are made in a manner that isn't too disruptive. Discussions also facilitate innovation by encouraging team members to open their minds to varied possibilities. Continuous dialogue encourages continuous learning, as your team members share their knowledge and problem-solving tools. Besides that, both formal brainstorming meetings and informal dialogue allow you and your team to ask the big "what-if?" questions. Dialogue creates space to speculate and imagine. It creates a space to think at different levels.

While meetings, brainstorming sessions, and problem-solving gatherings are important, never lose sight of their final purpose: helping you get things done. While you want to make adjustments and solve problems, don't process the issues to death. There is a point at which you have to get off the meeting carousel. There is a time when you need to stop talking and start acting.

Your challenge is to terminate meetings before everyone gets discouraged and burned out while retaining your credibility. As you move ahead, keep the sources of credibility in mind—for you, for your idea, and for your group. Be careful not to end the meeting process abruptly. Let your team know that you want to keep a problem-solving mind-set but that you want to move on to the next phase of execution.

Having leadership agility is about knowing when the dialogue has gone far enough and reining it in. When should you put a meeting to stop and declare a decision? When the core themes are being endlessly repeated; when criticisms are being made for the sake of filling air space; and when the inevitability of certain decisions has become obvious. Sometimes pragmatic leadership is about acknowledging that the discussion must come to an end—and ending it.

As an agenda mover, you need to understand that never-ending dialogue is as unproductive as no dialogue at all. You need to recognize when discussions have turned into overprocessing—that is, when the octopus has taken control. That's when you need to pound the gavel and say, "We're not meeting on this item again. We're moving ahead."

Be Smart about Resources

If you want your campaign to achieve results, it might come down to the question of resources. An agenda mover has to roll up his or her sleeves and deal with the issue of resources.

One of your responsibilities as a pragmatic agenda mover is to make sure that your team has the resources it needs. The lack of resources can kill the most motivated of campaigns. That said, an agenda mover understands that resources are finite. You can't throw every dollar at a project. You can't give people all the support they would have in an ideal world. The organizational truth is that supporting one project often means diverting resources from other projects. In making sure that key projects have the resources needed to go the distance, you have to prioritize.

If there is more than one project on your agenda, you have to prioritize. Prioritization also has to happen within projects. Everything costs money. With limited funds, where are you going to spend it? In the former case—i.e., if you need to weigh one project against another—you may be tempted to put most of your available resources into the more important project. You may reason that if you provide that team with ample resources, their creativity will flourish, and they will come up with groundbreaking new ideas. Certainly, having access to sufficient resources will improve your team's sense of possibility. Although not a guarantee of performance, having the sense that the needed materials, services, staff, and equipment are within reach will improve their commitment to your initiative.

An opposing school of thought says that if leaders deliberately limit the resources available to team members, they'll become more inventive. They may come up with better and more cost-effective solutions than if they had unlimited resources. Many managers find this an attractive philosophy, but it is risky. What happens if your team fails to come up with resource-lean solutions? What if the constraints on resources are so tight that it puts the goals of the coalition in danger?

Leaders often err on the side of too much cost cutting. Too much belt-tightening can undermine the progress of your most important projects. What happens if you have to tell your design team that there are no funds for new computers—while their industry peers are already using the latest hardware? When people feel they don't have access to the resources they need to do their job, their enthusiasm will flag. They may rethink their commitment to you and your agenda.

To sustain momentum and move your agenda ahead, you have to make sure, as much as you can, that everyone has the tools they need. Providing sufficient resources can be a tough decision for leaders who are also managing pressures from bosses, leaders, and shareholders, but consider the long-term effects of a leader like Mark Hurd, former CEO of Hewlett-Packard. Hurd was obsessed with efficiency, famously cutting costs across the company to triple profits from 2005 to 2009, faster than the rate of sales growth. Although this focus on operational efficiency was well received by investors, Hurd is rumored to have reduced research and development spending from 9 percent of revenue to 2 percent, leaving Hewlett-Packard without a response to the iPad and other technologies.[1] Agenda movers who are focused on the long-term will remember that although

Mark Hurd may have satisfied investors in the short term, operational excellence is not a substitute for innovation and growth.[2]

Your team needs the right tools to do the job, but you don't want them to take advantage of the system or get used to luxuries. You don't want the team's main purpose—that is, working on your agenda—to be superseded by finagling for better equipment or additional perks. This happens all the time in organizations. Money gets used for mysterious purposes. If you ask about these expenditures, it seems that no one knows who is using the resources or why.

As an agenda mover, you need to make sure your group's access to organizational resources doesn't fall below a certain threshold—from "hungry" to "discouraged." There is no science here. There are no quantitative metrics. You have to be intuitive and sensitive to your group's level of motivation and creativity. Sometimes the best way to find out if everyone is all right with their access to resources is to ask them. You may wish your team could work on vapors, but this isn't practical. You cannot afford to be insensitive to their needs.

Balance the allocation of resources. Don't vacillate between feast and famine. Find the sweet spot where your team has the resources it needs to move ahead but isn't raiding the storehouse. You can be both facilitative and directive in this matter. Facilitate what they need, and scrutinize what they want.

Define Parameters
Sometimes projects fall apart and momentum dies simply because no one is sure who is in charge. Either no one is making decisions—or everyone is, resulting in ongoing and contentious battles for turf. In moving your project forward, you will need to determine how much autonomy to give your team. You will need to figure out how to let them do their jobs without interfering too much and also how

143

to make sure they actually do their jobs.

You may be tempted to say, "Let them get it done, and I'll review it once it's complete." But what if it doesn't get done? What if they drop the ball? What if they procrastinate, or go off on detours? A classic example of misplaced autonomy is when President Obama first charged Congress with developing and passing a health care bill. The president kept his distance and thought that Congress would come through. But as it turned out, the president was too removed from the daily work of getting the bill written and passed, and no progress was made until he took a more hands-on role.

As an agenda mover, you'll need to know when to be hands-on and when to be hands-off. You need to be confident that your team knows where you're headed and can be trusted to deal with the details. To ensure this, give your team autonomy—but take time to define the parameters. Autonomy is best given when you and all your team members share a common understanding of where you're going and how you intend to get there. To reinforce the common direction, make sure to check in on a timetable that works not only for you (to get a pulse on what's going on) but also for them (to remind them that you're in their corner).

No one was more successful in laying out parameters than Sam Walton. Walton took time to articulate his vision. He was explicit in how he wanted his retail empire to operate, from product procurement to checkout. Within this framework, Walton understood that the key to success was to give his staff and managers the right amount of autonomy, such that they would feel ownership of the project. His mantra was, "Give folks responsibility."[3] Walton called his style "management by walking and flying around"[4]—literally: As he built his Walmart empire Walton would fly over towns in a small plane to scout locations for new stores, and he would walk through stores to see what was going on. Walton made it his business to know whether his employees were using their autonomy within his articulated parameters. He was able to balance autonomy with oversight without having to resort to micromanagement.

Autonomy, when practiced with concrete parameters, is positive for all concerned. Problems arise when leaders grant their team autonomy but send mixed messages. William Bradford Shockley, the brilliant engineer at Bell Labs and winner of the 1956 Nobel Prize in Physics, was notorious for his informality and hands-off style. He was, after all, a scientist, who valued the freedom of ideas. In 1956, Shockley assembled a group of talented young scientists and engineers and launched the Shockley Semiconductor Laboratory. But unlike Walton, Shockley set no parameters. Rather, he managed by capriciousness. No one knew what to expect. Sure, they had autonomy, but at any moment a new dictate, rule, or whim would overwhelm whatever work they could accomplish. It wasn't long before eight of Shockley's smartest young researchers went off on their own to form Fairfield Semiconductors; later, the same group founded Intel. Shockley thought he had given his team everything they wanted and felt betrayed when they left. Ever after, he referred to them as "the traitorous eight."[5]

Shockley forgot one of the primary lessons of pragmatic leadership—when sustaining momentum, give autonomy but specify the parameters. This is a fundamental leadership problem. Too loose and you run the risk of uncontrolled chaos. Too tight and you'll drive them to resent you. You need to strike a balance.

Bolster the Campaign Mind-set

In trying to get things done, agendas movers sometimes lose focus on maintaining a continued campaign mind-set. You've spent so much energy on moving your ideas and mobilizing people around them that you may forget that the campaign mind-set that rallied around your agenda remains critical to ensuring that the agenda is implemented. It's often said that once elected, politicians lose the mind-set that brought them into office.

As you move forward trying to actually get things done, your challenge is to sustain your team's collective sense of purpose. Agenda movers appreciate that the energy generated during the early stages of a project can fade when the drudgery of reality sinks in. Your challenge is to make sure that the psychological sense of purpose stays alive. When start-ups fail, sometimes it's not because the original intent or idea was invalid but because the team lost the collective energy that brought them together. An agenda mover knows how to manage the campaign mind-set.

A campaign mind-set is an energizing force. A group of individuals can work together at the same time, in the same office, and on the same project, but if they don't maintain the spirit that brought them together, they will become demoralized and lose their ability to sustain momentum. To go the distance, your team must act with a collective purpose. It's your job to make sure everyone stays on board.

A campaign mind-set is an energizing force that can cohere a group of individuals—from different units at the same geographic location or scattered across the globe—and get them working on the same project. If the campaign mind-set is missing, if team members don't feel a shared sense of purpose, a wider commitment, and a collective mission, then they will lose sight of the initial vision and forget about the first spark that made them so driven and motivated in the first place.

You can sustain the campaign mind-set by reminding them why they're part of your effort, reinforcing the payoff, keeping an optimistic outlook, and maintaining your credibility.

Remind Them Why They're Here

Somewhere along the way moving complex agendas can become difficult and mundane. Daily tasks and repetitive chores can make you feel like you're treading water. You feel like you are wearing blinders and can only see what's in front of you. There is some forward movement, but it feels like the road ahead only gets longer and the journey more dangerous.

Sure you make progress, but you can't shake the feeling that you're going nowhere fast. While it may appear you accomplished some tasks the truth is you're not much farther ahead then you were a week ago. If you feel like this, there's a good chance those in your coalition feel that way too. In this case, you need to sustain the campaign mind-set to get everyone remotivated. But vision and ideas aren't enough to sustain the campaign mind-set. Agenda movers need to remind their allies of their shared long-term goals.

Reminding your allies why they're there rejuvenates and recharges your effort. People want to be emotionally engaged and have a sense of purpose. A little reminder about why they become involved in the first place will help you rally your people. It is crucial to remind people not only about the importance of the mission but also about how important they are to the mission.

Reinforce the Payoff

As an agenda mover, you have to remind those working on your campaign what's in it for them. Those who have bought into your agenda believe in its virtues, but they are also hoping that their investment of time will reap some rewards.

It is normal for people to expect some benefit from joining your cause. After all, who hasn't wondered, "What can I get out of this?" People will remain invested in your agenda if they can perceive the payback they will receive. You can assume that as long as you are showing the real benefits from time to time then your people will stay in your corner and help push your agenda.

It is also your task to make sure no one supporting you is being perceived as a free rider, that is, someone who expects to benefit from an idea without actually investing a great deal of time or effort.

To sustain the campaign mind-set you have to show that you can provide resources and support your team. Reinvigorating the message will increase motivation, but reminding your people about the bottom line will keep them in the game.

Keep an Optimistic Outlook

Sustaining the campaign mind-set also revolves around keeping an optimistic outlook. As an agenda mover, you don't have to shy away from the facts. You can admit that obstacles and barriers are everywhere—but you also have to show your team that if they stick together they can get through anything.

Unpracticed leaders are prone to sinking into negative self-reflection and doubt, and they compound the error by sharing their misgivings and worries in a misguided effort to create a bond of trust and companionship with their people. They'll overshare their headaches and worries and yet still hope for success. That is unlikely to happen. Agenda movers should check their doubts and reaffirm their goals and ideas.

But that doesn't mean you have to be a senseless cheerleader. You can and should give the facts straight, but you have to show that every setback is an opportunity and that every problem is a challenge.

Failing to be optimistic will sap energy from the campaign and create more doubters, skeptics, and cynics who will help to create a self-fulfilling prophecy.

Maintain Your Credibility

The campaign mind-set can be sustained if your people believe in not only your ideas but also in you. Agenda movers have to illustrate their credibility so their people can believe that they have the ability to actually get things done.

To maintain a campaign mind-set you have to show that you have what it takes to move each part of your agenda forward. Still you have to keep in mind that credibility is earned; it is not bought, demanded, or bribed, and having it won't make people agree with every one of your ideas or initiatives. Yet without credibility you will have trouble keeping the lights on.

Right out of the gate you might earn credibility by creating a forward-thinking agenda, but as you encounter setbacks and attend to the day-to-day aspects of getting things done your credibility may take a nosedive. Every stumble and misstep will make your people wonder if you have what it takes to go the distance.

It is important to remember that credibility is precarious and often fluctuates. As an agenda mover you must make sure you sustain your credibility by accomplishing some tasks and by showing that you alone have what it takes to execute.

Stay Politically Astute

Generally, agenda movers are very astute and understand what it takes to get people on board. They can deftly deal with opposition, be savvy about splinter groups, naysayers, and political infighting, and be sensitive to coalitions. But, the peculiar thing is that the very political astuteness that they applied in leading the campaign is something that they forget when trying to sustain the campaign to actually get things done.

These individuals don't quite go the distance because they fail to continue to apply the political competence that got them this far. The two fundamental errors they make are to assume consensus too early and to view the implementation of their agenda as inevitable. They fail to realize that consensus is fickle, and agendas are never inevitable. Nothing can be considered implemented until it is actually implemented. It takes drive and continued political astuteness to make sure that your agenda is put in place.

If you want to get something done it is essential that that you use your astuteness to sustain political cohesion. This isn't always easy in the face of challenges, frustration, and burnout. The best of teams will encounter criticism and opposition, splinter groups, naysayers, and political infighting. Even those who most believe in your effort, who are most in your corner, will flounder once in a while.

There are two things that you must keep in mind: Don't feed the Trojan horse and beware of counter-coalitions. As you move toward getting things done, you can flounder because of internal conflict or external opposition. Your challenge is to deal with both.

Don't Feed the Trojan Horse

To effectively manage your team, you need to deal directly with any conflict that represents a challenge to the collective interest. You may overlook rumbles of dissent because you're concerned that dealing with dissatisfaction may threaten your coalition. You may not realize that the group with which you started your initiative may not be the group that you need now. To sustain momentum, you will need to revisit who is on your side and whom you want to keep on your side.

Although dissent and debate are a necessary part of the dynamics of any creative team, be wary. Remember the danger of the Trojan horse.

A Trojan horse can come in many colors. There are several general types:

The deceiver. This individual is externally cooperative, but at the same time, he or she is pursuing other agendas that may weaken or even subvert the team's efforts.

The toxic player. Again, the individual is externally cooperative and claims to be working for the good of the team—but his or her personality or style generates conflict and irritation.

The controller. This person is supersmooth and confident, and his or her abilities outshine those of other team members—but ultimately, by failing to work well with others, he or she weakens the team rather than strengthens it.

The hanger-on. This type clings to the past experience and direction of the organization but has trouble working toward new concepts, agendas, and directions.

Each of these types represents a potential Trojan horse. Externally, they seem to be an asset to the team, but beneath the veneer, their presence can be disruptive.

If Trojan horses were consciously Machiavellian, self-serving, and unscrupulous, then organizational life would be simpler for leaders. The problem is that Trojan horses have some positive attributes, and outwardly, their presence seems to be an asset to the team. Over time, however, their negative impact outweighs whatever virtues they bring to the project. When Trojan horses do more harm than good, pragmatic leaders must stop feeding them.

You may have spotted a Trojan horse on your team. The challenge is that others might not assess the situation the same way. When you let the Trojan horse go, others may accuse you of being capricious, vindictive, or downright stupid. You will be open to these charges because others may not see the subtle negatives that you do. In this instance, leadership is a question of courage; and it takes courage to stop feeding the Trojan horse.

During the 1960 election, John F. Kennedy struggled with choosing his running mate. His selection of Lyndon Johnson—an acknowledged archrival and a person whose personality and style were not closely aligned with Kennedy's—struck many, including Robert Kennedy, as a dangerous choice. The fear was that bringing Johnson into the administration would create a Trojan horse that could potentially undermine the cohesion needed to govern. The truth was that Kennedy needed Johnson's support for the general election, and he had no choice but to make him the VP candidate. However, once elected, Kennedy and his advisors worked to isolate Johnson to reduce the possibility of Johnson damaging the administration from the inside. For the most part, the move was a success in making sure that Johnson could, at the very least, do no harm.

The assassination of JFK led to another example of the Trojan horse phenomenon. Johnson decided to keep Robert Kennedy on as attorney general because it would have been unseemly to dismiss the late president's brother. The two men did not get along, they were contemptuous of each other, and their political styles were irreconcilable. Kennedy resigned to run for the senate seat of New York, but President Johnson felt he had to keep Kennedy in the fold and supported his campaign politically and personally. Some historians believe that RFK was a Trojan horse who contributed to the fall of the Johnson administration—but others believe that the care Johnson took not to alienate Kennedy prevented him from becoming a Trojan horse.

Agenda movers must know when to let someone go. They have to learn to admit, which at the time may not seem completely rational, when someone is not a great fit for the team. The issue is exemplified by the Ewing theory, named after the talented basketball player Patrick Ewing. Sportswriter Bill Simmons and his friend Dave Cirilli developed a theory to explain why Ewing's team always performed better when the star was injured or after he had moved on.[6]

When an athlete like Ewing receives a lot of attention from the media and fans but doesn't lead the team to victory, everyone blames the team, not the star. However, when the team meets or exceeds expectations without the star, it suddenly becomes clear that the star wasn't actually vital to the team. These underperforming stars are Trojan horses because they are touted as high performers, but by keeping everyone's attention on themselves, they actually detract from the team's ability to work together toward its goals.

Like a good basketball coach, agenda movers need to be mindful of talent that drags down the team.

It's difficult to take on a Trojan horse. It's much easier to ignore them or to assume that they'll come round. The problem is that Trojan horses may have a lot of backers on the team. When you decide to remove a Trojan horse, you have to make it clear to others that their removal will strengthen the team and that you are not acting out of jealousy or on the basis of some momentary whim or incidental irritation. Dealing with the Trojan horse is a pragmatic decision that must be based on your strong belief that its removal will enhance your team's cohesion and ability to move forward.

Beware of Counter-Coalitions

You don't need everyone in your coalition to agree with you all the time. Indeed, a key attribute of the pragmatic leader is an ability to listen to others, accept legitimate criticism, and live with a modicum of loyal dissent on certain issues. At the same time, you don't want to let people loose and have them form counter-coalitions. Internal opposition is one thing, but it's quite another to let a splinter group grow into a full-fledged enemy force.

You know that you will have naysayers. There will always be those who will say to your face—or to others behind your back—that your idea is weak or that you're missing the point. You can tell yourself they won't do much damage, but they can. You have to monitor your opposition so they don't gather enough strength to form a splinter group. Splinter groups may expand their agenda, gain momentum, and become active counter-coalitions. Having to deal with a counter-coalition puts you in a defensive position, forcing you to react to—or accommodate—their emerging agenda.

Take the emergence of the Tea Party, a loose confederation of political groups that are generally conservative in nature but whose interests and outlook deviate from the mainstream Republican Party. The Tea Party started as a motley collection of splinter groups and emerged as an active counter-coalition.

Larry Summers is a great example of a leader who ignored counter-coalitions at his peril and lost his presidency at Harvard University. Summers started his Harvard career with strong support from the university's faculty but soon made several controversial statements and decisions. After he made remarks implying that women are underrepresented in science and engineering leadership positions due to differences between men and women in "intrinsic aptitude,"[8] an already frustrated faculty almost immediately formed an anti-Summers counter-coalition. Their movement picked up momentum and media attention, distracting Summers from working on his other presidential tasks, such as fundraising. Summers assumed that any opposition would come from the usual suspects (i.e., a small group of disgruntled faculty) and that his leadership would be able to withstand any challenge. He was wrong.

A fictional example illustrates how failing to meet legitimate criticism forthrightly can balloon into the emergence of a counter-coalition. Consider a software firm that specializes in supporting administrative activities for public-sector organizations—e.g., local governments, schools, and public safety units. The company's software can be tweaked to meet a variety of client needs, from basic administration to customer service. Through acquisitions, the company has built a catalog of nearly one hundred products. Now it is faced with the problem of integrating its many acquisitions. The company wants to move from a product-based agenda to a solution-based one. It wants to sell customers solutions instead of specific products and hardware.

The firm's CFO decides to work with an external consultant to integrate the company's various products into a package that would give clients a unified solution for their administrative needs rather than offering a menu of software. Every department he meets with vows their cooperation, and the CFO feels that things are moving in a positive direction. But in the course of holding preliminary meetings, the CFO overlooks the urban government sales division (UGSD). While not the largest division, the UGSD makes a significant contribution to the organization. By not dealing with the UGSD early, the CFO unwittingly leaves space for them to become a counter-coalition. Members of the UGSD became strident in their support of the product-based approach—the approach that the CFO is working hard to move away from. As the CFO keeps hammering away at the solution-based model, the UGSD persuades other divisions that a solution-based approach will not carry the day. The CFO's team begins to fray.

In keeping your team together, bear in mind that counter-coalitions can come from anywhere, either internally or externally. Internally they can grow from an undetected Trojan horse. Externally they can begin with opposition from another department, another group, or another market sector.

While you need to be aware of splinter groups and potential counter-coalitions, however, it's equally important to remember that overreacting to potential counter-coalitions can be as damaging as failing to notice their existence. If you become obsessive about potential opposition groups, you risk losing direction and focus. You will end up spending more time responding to opposition groups than working on your own agenda—and so will your team. In extreme cases, as you lose your way, the arguments of a counter-coalition can start to sound attractive to your team.

It's your job, as an agenda mover, to recognize interest groups, splinter groups, and counter-coalitions, and respond to their presence appropriately. As always, finding the right balance is delicate but necessary to sustain your team's momentum.

▲ ▲ ▲

Don't drop the ball. It is one thing to get elected, one thing to gain the buy-in of others. Now you have to get things done, and you need to establish some degree of traction by creating small victories and getting validation of your ideas. Traction gives your agenda and your supporters not only a sense of the possible but also the reassurance that there is concrete movement.

As you try to get things done, you need to be guarded against inertia. You need to make sure that the forward moment is sustained, and that means juggling your leadership style, controlling the dialogue, and always bolstering the campaign mind-set. Leaders who drift away from their original agenda often find their initiatives becoming stuck or stalled. Focus is key to sustaining momentum. You have to be concerned with keeping your team optimistic and maintaining the credibility of your agenda. Last, you have to be constantly aware that that even though you're moving ahead, there may be a political challenge around the corner in the form of a Trojan horse or a counter-coalition.

CONCLUSION

"We" Not "I": You Can't Do It Alone

While there is perpetual discussion among academics and practitioners deliberating what leadership is all about, this book is predicated on the simple assumption that if you cannot move your agenda, you are not a leader. In the final analysis, leadership is about getting things done. It's not simply about your ideas or your personality; it is about your capacity to take your ideas and work them through the maze of resistance, overcome challenges, and put those ideas in place. Leaders are remembered for their accomplishments, not their promises.

In all arenas, innovation and change are dependent on agenda movers. In a culture in which everything is packaged in terms of drama, vision, and promises, we often lose sight of what it really takes to move an agenda ahead. Agenda movers understand what it takes to move things forward. They appreciate the tenacity, agility, and skills necessary to get things done. They realize that having a good idea or an abundance of personality is not enough. They know that learning the practical skills of leadership will take their intention to success. As an agenda mover, you need to develop an awareness of your grounded reality, a clear focus on what needs to be done, and an understanding of what can and cannot be accomplished.

The core message of this volume is straightforward—try to be mindful of where you want to go and whose support you will need to help you get there. There is an implicit message throughout this book—an agenda mover knows that he or she cannot do it alone. Successful agenda movers rarely use the word "I"—instead, they use the word "we." They talk about "what we can accomplish" or "what we can do together." When you use "we," you empower the other party or parties involved. When you use "I," you underline your sense of power and importance to the process. The agenda mover realizes the symbolic and real power of the word "we."

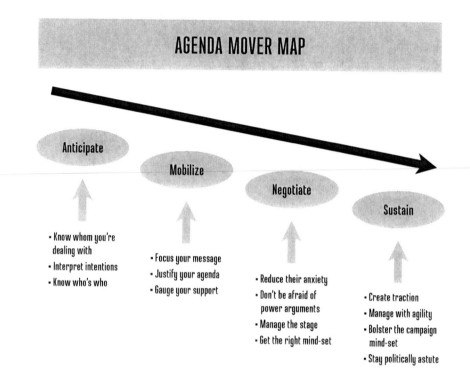

AGENDA MOVER MAP

Anticipate
- Know whom you're dealing with
- Interpret intentions
- Know who's who

Mobilize
- Focus your message
- Justify your agenda
- Gauge your support

Negotiate
- Reduce their anxiety
- Don't be afraid of power arguments
- Manage the stage
- Get the right mind-set

Sustain
- Create traction
- Manage with agility
- Bolster the campaign mind-set
- Stay politically astute

Consequently, keep your focus not simply on your intentions and aspirations but also on the intentions and aspirations of others. That means to first anticipate the agendas of others: know where they are coming from; understand their inclinations; and delve into their agenda. In that context, you need to anticipate not only their cooperation but also their hesitation and possible resistance.

Having anticipated the agendas of others, you now must mobilize your campaign. Get their initial support. Win them to your side. You must focus your message, justify your agenda, enhance your credibility, and be mindful of the type of support you would like from them. Having launched your message and gained some initial support, you need to get the buy-in, that is, explicit support and a deeper commitment that will allow you to go the distance. You must address their concerns and anxieties, and let them know what they can gain. And if the situation demands it, you can use powerful arguments to make explicit the benefits of your agenda. You need to manage the stage as the backdrop to your negotiation of the buy-in.

Now that you have the support, you have to get things done. You have to ensure that the campaign is sustained to get results. You don't want to drop the ball or walk away just because you have initial support. You want to make sure that your agenda is put in place. And that means creating traction, managing with agility, bolstering the campaign mind-set, and staying politically astute.

Throughout this campaign, it is essential that you keep in mind one thing: You need the support of others. Failed leaders are those who assume that they are the most important player. You may be important but only as long as others believe in you and are willing to work with you.

Often the question is asked: Are leaders born, or can they be trained? Over the years, my colleagues at BLG and I have trained many leaders in numerous organizations. There is always the one individual who comes to these trainings with the sense that they are not a leader. I recall when a senior engineer working on an R&D team at a major multinational corporation came to a training session. His team was working on innovations that they thought were valuable. The team was capable of getting their ideas almost to the point of prototype, but when they needed to secure financial backing to take the project to the next level, they continuously fell short. Coming into the training, the engineer failed to appreciate that he was playing in a political arena, with resource restrictions and competing agendas. He gave little credence to the hard work necessary to gain support so something could actually get done. With this insight, he was able to approach his role with a different mind-set. If you want to lead innovation and change, you have to drive through the eye of needle. You have to convince them, win them over, and go the distance. It requires focused behavior, but this behavior can be learned. You can master the skills of the agenda mover from reading, training, and continuous practice.

I hesitate to leave you with the notion that this volume or any of our trainings can guarantee your success. That said, I am sure that mastering these core skills will go a long way toward helping your ideas see the light of day. The key is practice, practice, practice.

Notes

1. THE POLITICAL COMPETENCE OF EXECUTION

1. "Twitter Cofounder Jack Dorsey's Advice to Innovators," CBS News, March 6, 2012, accessed February 9, 2016, http://www.youtube.com/watch?feature=player_embedded&v=V76ey3Ug8pM.

2. Paul Farhi, "Jeffrey Bezos, Washington Post's Next Owner, Aims for a New 'Golden Era' at the Newspaper," *Washington Post*, September 2, 2013, accessed January 10, 2014, https://www.washingtonpost.com/lifestyle/style/jeffrey-bezos-washington-posts-next-owner-aims-for-a-new-golden-era-at-the-newspaper/2013/09/02/30c00b60-13f6-11e3-b182-1b3bb2eb474c_story.html.

3. Cited in David L. Cawthon, , "Leadership: The Great Man Theory Revisited," *Business Horizons*, May–June 1996, 1–4.

4. "Brown Puts Blame on Louisiana Officials," CNN, September 25, 2005, accessed February 9, 2016, http://www.cnn.com//2005/POLITICS/09/27/katrina.brown/index.html?section=cnn_topstories.

5. Mary Riddell, "If You Don't Like Geeks, You're in Trouble," *The Telegraph*, October 20, 2010, accessed February 9, 2016, http://www.telegraph.co.uk/technology/billgates/8073946/Bill-Gates-If-you-dont-like-geeks-youre-in-trouble.html.

6. R. Alton Lee, *Eisenhower and Landrum-Griffin: A Study in Labor-Management Politics* (Lexington: University Press of Kentucky, 1990), viii.

7. Richard E. Dauch, *American Drive: How Manufacturing Will Save Our Country* (New York: St. Martin's Press, 2012), 79.

8. Stephen E. Ambrose, The Victors: *Eisenhower and His Boys: The Men of World War II* (New York: Simon & Schuster,1999), 22.

9. Samuel Bacharach, "Leadership without Presumptions: Lessons from Eisenhower," *Inc.*, June 26, 2016, accessed September 11, 2014, http://www.inc.com/samuel-bacharach/leadership-without-presumption-lessons-from-eisenhower.html.

10. Ian Burrell, "Mark Zuckerberg: He's Got the Whole World on His Site," *The Independent*, July 23, 2010, accessed September 14, 2014, http://www.independent.co.uk/news/people/profiles/mark-zuckerberg-hes-got-the-whole-world-on-his-site-2034134.html.

11. David Kirkpatrick, "The Second Coming of Apple," CNN Money/Fortune, November 9, 1988, accessed September 15, 2014, http://money.cnn.com/magazines/fortune/fortune_archive/1998/11/09/250834/.

12. Martin Luther King Jr., "Domestic Impact of the War" (speech), National Labor Assembly for Peace, November 1967, accessed August 10, 2014, http://www.aavw.org/special_features/speeches_speech_king03.html.

13. Arthur Padilla, *Portraits in Leadership: Six Extraordinary University Presidents* (Westport, CT: Praeger, 2005), 3.

14. Lenny Bernstein, "Eight-State Coalition Plans Incentives for Zero Emission Vehicles," *Washington Post*, October 24, 2014, Accessed November 1, 2014, https://www.washingtonpost.com/national/health-science/eight-state-coalition-plans-incentives-for-zero-emission-vehicles/2013/10/24/f79b36f8-3ca3-11e3-a94f-b58017bfee6c_story.html.

15. Matthew L. Wald, "8 States Teaming Up to Support Electric Cars," *New York Times*, October 24, 2013, accessed November 1, 2014, http://www.nytimes.com/2013/10/25/business/energy-environment/coalition-of-states-seeks-to-spur-use-of-electric-cars.html.

2. ANTICIPATE THE AGENDAS OF OTHERS

1. Anupreeta Das, "Buffett's Crisis-Lending Haul Reaches $10 Billion," *Wall Street Journal*, October 6, 2013, accessed January 14, 2014, http://online.wsj.com/news/articles/SB10001424052702304441404579119742104942198.

2. Henry Ford, *My Life and Work* (New York: Doubleday, 1922), 72.

3. Andrew Salmon, "Samsung's Mr. TV," Forbes, March 31, 2011, accessed January 15, 2016, http://www.forbes.com/global/2011/0411/features-yoon-boo-keun-tv-3d-led-samsung-battle.html.

4. Bonnie Feldman, "Multiple Myeloma Research Foundation: One Person's Power to Ignite Collaboration," The Doctor Weighs In, July 7, 2014, accessed January 15, 2016, http://thedoctorweighsin.com/multiple-myeloma-research-foundation-one-persons-power-ignite-collaboration/.

5. Bill George, "America's Best Leaders: Anne Mulcahy, Xerox CEO," *U.S. News & World Report*, November 19, 2008, accessed January 12, 2013, http://www.usnews.com/news/best-leaders/articles/2008/11/19/americas-best-leaders-anne-mulcahy-xerox-ceo.

6. Reed Hastings, "How I Did It: Reed Hastings, Netflix," *Inc.*, December 5, 2005, accessed June 1, 2013, http://www.inc.com/magazine/20051201/qa-hastings.html.

7. Peter Cohan, "How to Become a Master of Adaptation," *Inc.* October 23, 2013, accessed August 31, 2014, http://www.inc.com/peter-cohan/3-start-up-lessons-from-netflix-master-of-adaptation.html.

8. James B. Stewart, "Netflix Looks Back on Its Near-Death Spiral," *New York Times*, April 26, 2013, accessed August 31, 2014, http://www.nytimes.com/2013/04/27/business/netflix-looks-back-on-its-near-death-spiral.html.

9. Brad Tuttle, "Can the Boutique 'Store-within-a-Store' Concept Save Big Box Retailers from Extinction?" *Time*, April 8, 2013, accessed January 14, 2016, http://business.time.com/2013/04/08/can-the-boutique-store-within-a-store-concept-save-big-box-retailers-from-extinction/.

10. Meghan Foley, "Was J.C. Penney Wounded by Johnson's Mass Layoffs?" *Cheat Sheet*, April 15, 2013, accessed January 15, 2016, http://www.cheatsheet.com/business/stock-news/was-j-c-penney-wounded-by-johnsons-mass-layoffs.html.

3. MOBILIZE YOUR CAMPAIGN

1. George M. Fredrickson, *Big Enough to Be Inconsistent: Abraham Lincoln Confronts Slavery and Race* (Cambridge: Harvard University Press, 2008), 86.
2. Treatment Action Group, biography of Mark Harrington, Executive Director, accessed November 15, 2014, http://www.treatmentactiongroup.org/staff/mark-harrington.
3. Bruce Weber, "Spencer Cox, Aids Activist, Dies at 44," New York Times, December 21, 2012, accessed November 15, 2013, http://www.nytimes.com/2012/12/21/nyregion/spencer-cox-aids-activist-dies-at-44.html.

4. NEGOTIATE SUPPORT

1. "A Record-Breaking Feat," *Best Practice*, February 2013, accessed January 15, 2016, http://www.t-systems.com/news-media/shell-pulls-off-the-largest-sap-upgrade-in-history-now-its-mobile-collaboration-tools-are-delivered-from-a-private-cloud-t-systems/1100966.
2. Ibid.
3. "Chrysler CEO on Company's Remarkable Turnaround," *CBS News*, March 23, 2003, accessed January 12, 2016, http://www.cbsnews.com/news/chrysler-ceo-on-companys-remarkable-turnaround/.
4. Robert A. Caro, "LBJ Goes for Broke," *Smithsonian Magazine*, June 2002, accessed January 12, 2016,
5. Robert A. Caro, *The Years of Lyndon Johnson: The Passage of Power* (New York: Knopf, 2012), xv.
6. "The Lyndon B. Johnson White House Recordings: Overview," The Miller Center, University of Virginia, accessed January 15, 2016, http://millercenter.org/presidentialrecordings/johnson/about.
7. Tom Wicker, "Remembering the Johnson Treatment," *The New York Times*, May 9, 2002, accessed January 15, 2016, http://www.nytimes.com/2002/05/09/opinion/remembering-the-johnson-treatment.html.
8. Lawrence Wright, *Thirteen Days in September: Carter, Begin, and Sadat at Camp David* (New York: Knopf, 2014), 45.
9. James B. Stewart, "Eight Days," *The New Yorker*, September 21, 2009, accessed February 9, 2016, http://www.newyorker.com/magazine/2009/09/21/eight-days.

5. SUSTAIN YOUR CAMPAIGN

1. Joe Nocera, "Real Reason for Ousting H.P.'s Chief," New York Times, August 13, 2010, accessed January 15, 2016, http://www.nytimes.com/2010/08/14/business/14nocera.html?pagewanted=all.
2. August 11, 2010, accessed November 12, 2015, http://www.businessweek.com/magazine/content/10_34/b4192017461548.htm.
3. Richard S. Tedlow, Giants of Enterprise (New York: Harper Collins, 2009), 364.

4. Ibid., 364.

6. Ibid., 389.

7. Bill Simmons, "Ewing 101," ESPN, July 21, 2009, accessed January 23, 2016, http://proxy.espn.go.com/espn/page2/story?id=1193711.

8. Lawrence H. Summers, "Remarks at NBER Conference on Diversifying the Science & Engineering Workforce," Office of the President (Harvard), January 14, 2005, accessed March 29, 2016, http://www.harvard.edu/president/speeches/summers_2005/hber.php.

About the Bacharach Leadership Group:
Training for *Pragmatic Leadership*™

"Vision without execution is hallucination."—Thomas Edison

The litmus test of pragmatic leadership is results. The Bacharach Leadership Group (BLG) focuses on the skills necessary to lead and move agendas. Whether in corporations, nonprofits, universities, or entrepreneurial start-ups, BLG instructors train leaders in the core competencies necessary to execute change and innovation.

At all levels of the organization, leaders must master ideation skills for innovation, political skills for moving change, negotiation skills for building support, coaching skills for engagement, and team leadership skills for going the distance.

The BLG approach:

1. ASSESSMENT
BLG will assess your organizational challenges and leadership needs.

2. ALIGNMENT
BLG will align its training solutions with your organization's challenges and culture.

3. TRAINING
BLG training includes options for mixed-modality delivery, interactive activities, and collaboration with an emphasis on application.

4. OWNERSHIP
BLG provides continuous follow-up, access to the exclusive BLG mobile apps library, and coaching.

Whether delivering a complete leadership academy or a specific program or workshop, BLG will partner with you to get the results you need.

To keep up to date with the BLG perspective, visit blg-lead.com
or contact us at info@blg-lead.com.

About the BLG *Pragmatic Leadership*™ Series

In partnership with Cornell University Press, the Bacharach Leadership Group is introducing the BLG *Pragmatic Leadership* Series. These BLG-authored volumes focus on specific skills necessary to succeed in a constantly changing organizational world of networks, turf, and silos. The volumes in the BLG *Pragmatic Leadership* Series are practitioner orientated, but academically grounded, and emphasize the specific skills of execution that leaders at all levels of an organization need to master.

The second volume in the BLG *Pragmatic Leadership* Series is *Transforming the Clunky Organization: Leading for Discovery and Delivery*. Other volumes in the series will focus on leading with empathy, agile teams, and the leader as negotiator.

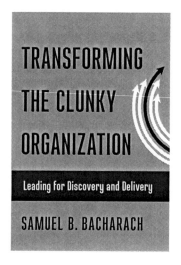

TRANSFORMING THE CLUNKY ORGANIZATION

Leading for Discovery and Delivery

SAMUEL B. BACHARACH

Keep the BLG *Pragmatic Leadership* Series on your radar!